FASHIONING
A HEALTHIER RELIGION

FASHIONING A HEALTHIER RELIGION

Thomas Aldworth, O.F.M.

THE THOMAS MORE PRESS
Chicago, Illinois

The author and publisher wish to thank the University of
Chicago Press for permission to include quotations from
Law, Sex and Christian Society by James A. Brundage.
Copyright 1987 by James A. Brundage.

ISBN 0-88347-273-2

CONTENTS

THOMAS P. ALDWORTH is a Franciscan priest who is the pastor of Saint Anthony Church in Parma, Ohio. He received his Masters of Divinity from Catholic Theological Union, Chicago, and his Masters in Counseling from Louisiana Tech University. He also holds a third degree black belt in the Korean martial art of tae kwon do. Most of his priesthood has been spent in parishes and campus ministry. His first book was *Shaping a Healthy Religion: Especially If You Are Catholic.*

Preface

FASHIONING A HEALTHIER RELIGION is a sequel
to *Shaping a Healthy Religion, Especially If You Are
Catholic*. There is no need, however, to be familiar with
the first book. The number of responses generated by
Shaping made me want to again turn my hand to
writing on religion. I've been a Franciscan for over
twenty-five years. I've been a priest in the Catholic
Church for over 18 years. Almost all that time has been
spent in various parish ministries. Sharing the joys
and sorrows of people in parishes has made me want
to be of whatever assistance I can be in shaping,
fashioning, a healthier religious perspective than the
one I was given.

I'm not a theologian. I'm a parish priest. I try to
make sense of what I've been taught and what I've
come to believe. I consider myself primarily a story-
teller, sharing the stories of my life and how they
speak to me of God's presence. I pray my stories will
speak to your heart and soul. I realize that some of
what I have written may strike people as being overly-
critical of the church. I hope, however, that my love

for the church may also be evident in my stories and in my struggles. My faith continues to seek understanding. May we seek such understanding together!

CHAPTER ONE

Divine Starting-Points

DURING my high school sophomore year, my older brother got married. Being a member of the bridal party, I got to dress up in a tuxedo. I had never worn a tuxedo. I felt foolish and grown-up simultaneously, a common occurrence of my adolescent years.

The wedding ceremony went well. Then came the reception. As a bridal party member, I was paired with a girl my own age, a cousin of the bride. After dinner, the band began to play and I knew I was in trouble. A new dance craze had recently stormed the country. Everyone was doing "the twist." But I didn't know how to twist. I knew some of the "old" dances but not this new one. Being considerably gangly, I realized how ungraceful I'd appear endeavoring to "twist". Rather than suffer such shame, I spent most of my brother's wedding reception in the bathroom.

I begin with this embarrassing episode because I believe being embarrassed has much to do with God and religion. As Rabbi Abraham Heschel tells us: "Religion depends upon what man does with his ultimate embarrassment." I'm not sure if God is embarrassed by me but I'm certainly embarrassed by God. Embarrassed and delighted at the same time. After all, doesn't Jeremiah 13:11 tell us we're as close to God as a loincloth? While it may be unsettling to envision ourselves as God's loincloth, as his "jockey shorts," I'm elated God allows such intimacy.

While being periodically embarrassed by God, I'm more often embarrassed for God. I'm constantly startled by what we say and do in his name. God's name is more often taken in vain to justify acquiescence to life's misfortunes than by cursing or swearing.

I recall a child's funeral that I attended in northern Louisiana. The funeral was at a Baptist church and I was there on behalf of the child's Catholic grandparents. The preacher began by announcing how wonderful it was that this child would not have to endure the "end times" (that apocalyptic favorite of fundamentalists). God had taken this child and put him on the other side of "the river" (I wasn't sure which river) so all of us would lead moral lives and get to heaven. God "took" this little one to dissuade us from immorality.

I was hard-pressed not to jump up and challenge the preacher. Recognizing the need for decorum, however, I sat in my seat and simmered. I wondered how such a sermon could be consoling. In the face of such tragedy, do we feel better depicting God as a child-

Fashioning a Healthier Religion

slayer? What kind of God snatches children from their families in order to dampen our immoral desires? Perhaps a God worth fearing but not a God worth worshipping. Sitting in that church, I was acutely embarrassed for God.

Such godly embarrassment often impels me to defend God from what is done in his name. I realize God is probably able to defend himself but he doesn't seem to be doing so. What if God is like the sweetheart whose honor we must occasionally defend? I'm sure if I had a "sweetie," I'd defend her name and honor with great vigor. My sweetheart would know the ardor implied in my willingness to jump into the breech for her honor. Perhaps part of my desire to "defend" God is actually my desire for God.

Mentioning sweethearts reminds me of my first dance. After my class' graduation from eighth grade back in 1961, we were allowed to attend the Friday night high school dance. Being able to attend our first real dance was something we all eagerly anticipated. I even asked a classmate of mine named Margaret Stevens to be my date. I nervously met Margaret at her house, a block from my own. After a brief parental evaluation, Margaret and I walked over to Leo High School on Chicago's Southside.

At the dance, the guys and girls separated. The guys clumped together at one end of the gym and the girls clustered at the other end. There weren't any "real"

Thomas Aldworth

high school students at the dance since they knew it would be flooded with grade school graduates. It would not be "cool" to be seen with us. So we were on our own; a gaggle of grade school graduates trying to appear worldly-wise.

The music started while we all stared across the dance floor at each other. After awhile, the girls shrugged their shoulders and began to dance with each other. We guys gazed on, uncertain how to cross the chasm between them and us. We lacked the courage to ask for a dance. We pretended to be enjoying our "manly" togetherness but we knew we were pretending.

After awhile, I began to feel guilty. I knew that since I had brought Margaret to the dance, I had some sort of moral obligation to dance with her. I was a moralist even at thirteen! So finally hitching up my pants, I crossed "no man's land" to dance with Margaret.

My comrades weren't far behind in venturing with their own trembling feet into the grace-full world of girls. Swept up in the sounds of Del Shannon, the Ventures, the Shirelles and the Four Seasons, we felt that night was our rite of passage from childhood to whatever came next. I had a most memorable evening doing my best not to step on Margaret's feet or trip on my own.

In the years since that June night, I've wondered if God is like those young girls who waited for us to

Fashioning a Healthier Religion

ask them to dance. What if God is waiting for us to cross over and ask for a dance? Yet many of us refuse to ask him not because we lack courage. We leave God a perpetual wall-flower because of the horrifying images we've been given of him. The God images flooding most of our souls make us certain we want little to do with him. The God who damns will find few who want to hold his hand or take a spin on a dance floor.

This hesitancy about God is linked with our experience of sinfulness. We find ourselves unsure about God because we fear our sins will "offend" him like some divinely perceptible body odor. We dread asking God to dance and having him say "no." Not many of us have self-identities strong enough to withstand being rebuffed by our Maker. We'd rather not ask than to risk a divine refusal. So we sit in our silence while God dances solo.

Dancing with someone can lead to love. Admittedly I'm not an expert on the link between dancing and love but I do know that feelings of love can escalate with the soft swaying of a slow waltz. Yet most of us aren't willing to waltz with God. We'd rather not fall in love with him. He may look good on the dance floor but we've heard he has a terrible temper. If we mistakenly step on his feet, his look alone might incinerate us. At least that's what we're led to believe if we take all of Scripture literally. The God of Genesis makes a lousy dance partner. I'd choose Margaret any day over the God who sulfurizes Sodom and Gomorrah.

Many of the God-distortions we encounter are connected with our understanding of Scripture. If we perceive Scripture as being magically written by God, then we cannot help but have warped images of God. Many of the God images raining down on us from the early books of Scripture drown our souls. How is it possible to have a passionate desire for the God of Noah and the Ark? Would anyone in their right mind want a romantic liaison with the Terminator God of the Torah?

Look, for instance, at the Noah story, which is one of the first stories about God we are taught as children. God is upset with what he has created so he petulantly decides to destroy all land-living creatures. Noah, however, finding favor with God, will be spared along with his family. He is commissioned to build a big boat in order to escape the wet wrath of God. Completing his task, Noah brings onto the ark *seven* pairs of all "clean" animals and *one* pair of the "unclean" animals. (Unclean animals were those who weren't supposed to be eaten, such as bats and pigs.) Sea-living creatures apparently weren't repulsive to God since they were spared the watery onslaught.

Anyway, the menagerie floats around while everything on land perishes. After the waters "had maintained their crest over the earth for one hundred and fifty days," God "remembered Noah and all the animals, wild and tame, that were with him in the ark." I suggested once in a homily that the reason God "remembered" probably had a lot to do with the Ark's aroma.

After the flood waters recede, Noah gets out of the ark. The first thing he does is set up an altar for the Lord "and choosing from every clean animal and every clean bird, he offered holocausts on the altar." (A good thing there was more than one pair of the clean animals!) When God smells "the sweet odor" of the burning animals, he decides not to destroy all land creatures again, at least not by water. I'm not too sure about the "sweet" smell of burning animals but maybe God has a weakness for barbecues?

We usually present the story of Noah and the Ark in a cute way to our little ones. We show them picture books with the animals going up the gangplank two-by-two. But perhaps the story wouldn't be so appealing if we showed Noah bringing the animals out, chopping them up and burning them on an altar. It's not exactly a bed-time story!

I've preached a few times on the Noah story. One Sunday in Ruston, Louisiana I got carried away. I was pacing up and down the aisle, getting excited by the theological implications of the story. I exclaimed how God had gotten "pissed off" and had decided

15

to destroy everything. Well, I certainly understood the consternation occasioned by my unfortunate language. The following Sunday I meekly apologized to those parishioners who had gotten "pissed off" because of my sermon on God being "pissed off."

Obviously, the God revealed in the Noah story is not the God I believe in. To desire a love affair with the God of Noah could only arise from a masochistic heart. I'd rather pet Cerberus, the Greek Hound of Hades, than venerate the vindictive God of Noah.

I don't want to particularly pick on Noah and his Ark. I use the story as an example of the God envisaged by Genesis. I certainly don't believe the story of Noah to be historically true. Yet there are many people who hold that all the stories contained in Scripture have to be historically true. They visualize Scripture as a large set of dominoes. If one story falls, then all of Scripture will come crashing down. While such a view may be curiously consoling, it makes no sense. The God of Noah cannot be embraced with either passion or intelligence. The God of Noah inhabits the nightmare world, rather than the world of historical reality.

Most of us were raised to believe that God is somehow the anonymous author of Scripture. We were taught to see Scripture as "The Word of God." We visualized God whispering the words of the Bible into someone's ear while he or she wrote it all down

Fashioning a Healthier Religion

in some sort of ancient shorthand. It's no wonder we feel like Alice in Wonderland when we approach Scripture.

In our church we believe that the Bible was "inspired" by God. Yet while we believe in such "inspiration," we haven't had much help understanding what it means. *The Jerome Biblical Commentary,* one of the main Catholic commentaries on the Bible, speaks of Scripture as something "which has been breathed by God—in other words, the very breath of God himself." Perhaps we can visualize inspiration as God "breathing" upon the authors of Scripture, helping them like sailboats to voyage further than they otherwise could. Some of the biblical writers were able to catch a great deal of breath in their sails, traveling great distances. Others, however, had sails which couldn't "catch" as much breath, so they didn't travel as far.

While all of Scripture should be taken together, like a giant mural, some of the "brush strokes" are rather strange. Look, for instance, at Deuteronomy 25:11: "When two men are fighting and the wife of one intervenes to save her husband from the blows of his opponent, if she stretches out her hand and seizes the latter by his private parts, you shall chop off her hand without pity." Perhaps a Biblical forerunner of the Marquess of Queensberry? Yet in all seriousness, can anyone imagine such an invective coming from God?

Thomas Aldworth

"You shall chop off her hand *without pity*." The God unveiled in the Gospels could not author such a devilish decree.

The hundreds of "commandments" (613 to be precise) found in the "Torah," or first five books of the Old Testament, make interesting reading but they truly strain belief in God as the one who wrote these books. Many of the laws have to do with preventing such diseases as Hansen's disease. There are also many proscriptions concerning blood. Since God's "life force" was somehow seen as being contained in blood (see Genesis 9:4), it was considered sacred to the Israelites. They couldn't eat anything with blood in it. They sacrificed animals to God because in slaughtering the animal, the blood was released and the "life force" returned to God. Men couldn't touch a menstruating woman (nor, for instance, sit on a chair she had sat upon) or else they would be considered ritually unclean.

Being "unclean" was a bad business. If a person was unclean, he or she would not be allowed into the temple or synagogue. God's protection was removed from anyone or anything rendered "unclean." God "protected" people only as long as they remained ritually clean. Without such "protection," a person was easy prey for all wandering unclean spirits and demons. God's "hand" could not "touch" anyone or anything unclean. So one had to be very careful

Fashioning a Healthier Religion

not to experience such ritual uncleanliness. A faithful Israelite, for instance, would never think of touching a woman on the street just in case that woman was menstruating. Any such touch would result in uncleanliness.

This concept of God's protection linked to the avoidance of uncleanliness is woven throughout the Books of Deuteronomy, Leviticus and Numbers. There are even proscriptions concerning nocturnal emissions and consequent military victory or defeat. As Deuteronomy 23:10-16 declares:

> When you are in camp during an expedition against your enemies, you shall keep yourselves from everything offensive. If one of you becomes ritually unclean because of a nocturnal emission, he shall go outside the camp and not return until, toward evening, he has bathed in water; then when the sun has set, he may come back into the camp. Outside the camp you shall have a place set aside to be used as a latrine. You shall also keep a trowel in your equipment and with it, when you go outside to ease nature, you shall first dig a hole and afterward cover up your excrement. Since the Lord, your God, journeys along with your camp to defend you and put your enemies at your mercy, your camp must be holy; *otherwise, if he sees anything indecent in your midst, he will leave your company.*

Uncleanliness and being defeated in battle were understood as theologically related. I wonder how many defeats were blamed on nocturnal emissions?

19

Thomas Aldworth

A goodly number of godly people proclaim everything in Scripture to be divine truth. They insist on a historical Adam and Eve. They demand a historical Noah and his floating zoo. Yet such good-intentioned people often cause others to turn from religion in frustration. Can we really believe "if a man lies in sexual intercourse with a woman during her menstrual period, both of them shall be cut off from their people" (Leviticus 20:18)? Can we imagine God being so concerned with the male sexual organ that "no man who has been castrated or whose penis has been cut off may be included among the Lord's people" (Deuteronomy 23:1)? Of course, those of us who are males might envision such a penis-focused God.

I admittedly have a tortuous time imagining a God who cares about men having sexual relations with menstruating women or women who grab for the groin in a fight. I cannot easily conceive a God who brings defeat upon people because of nocturnal emissions. However, I admit a personal bias concerning the 613 proscriptions of the Torah. Leviticus 19:27 proclaims: "Do not clip your hair at the temples, nor trim the edges of your beard." Having trimmed my beard for the past 15 years, I shudder to think of God keeping track of each trimming, adding it all up on my celestial scorecard.

Backtracking a bit, I'd like to say a few words about

the story of Adam and Eve. I believe the story of Adam and Eve is one of the most theologically and psychologically destructive stories ever written. Many of us were given our first taste of religion with this story. I'm afraid, though, that such a first taste destroyed many of our religious "taste buds."

Recall that Adam and Eve get thrown out of Eden not because they had disobeyed and eaten the fruit from the tree of the knowledge of good and evil. They get thrown out because God is jealous of immortality and doesn't wish to share it. Remember there were two trees whose fruit was forbidden. One was the tree of the knowledge of good and evil. The other was the tree of everlasting life. Since Adam and Eve had proven so bold as to eat from the one tree, God was afraid they would eat from the other tree and become like him. As Genesis 3:22 and 3:24 point out:

> Then the Lord God said: See! the man has become like one of us, knowing what is good and what is bad! Therefore, he *must not be allowed to put out his hand to take fruit from the tree of life also and thus eat of it and live forever.*
>
> When he expelled the man, he settled him east of the garden of Eden; and *he stationed the cherubim and the fiery revolving sword, to guard the way to the tree of life.*

So Adam and Eve wind up east of Eden because God selfishly guards immortality. The real mistake Adam

21

and Eve made was in not eating the fruit from the tree of everlasting life first.

One of the major problems with the Adam and Eve story is what is says about human creation. One of the probable reasons for the story's creation was to solve the theological dilemma of a perfect Creator and an imperfect creation. If God is perfect, couldn't he have done a better job in creating the universe? Where does suffering and death come from? How does evil arise? The Adam and Eve story argues that God created perfectly but that the first humans destroyed the perfection. Humans became God's scapegoat. Rather than blame our Maker, we decided to blame ourselves. A tremendous burden of guilt and shame has overshadowed us since.

The Adam and Eve story implies that God didn't intend for us to be the way we are, that he created us differently. Such a belief damages our souls at a profoundly deep level. We are not as God created us! Our proto-ancestors decided against perfection, choosing to risk disobedience. All the torments we suffer stem from that single act of disobedience. What a tremendous guilt trip we have undertaken! Rather than risk an imperfect Creator, we have fashioned ourselves as perpetually rebellious ingrates. Claiming God couldn't have made us this way, we have envisioned our conception as flawed.

Fashioning a Healthier Religion

Rather than imagine a defective deity, we have swallowed the shame as our own.

I believe we are the way we are precisely because God wanted us to be this way. We are created as we are because our Creator wished us to be created in just such a manner. While I may not fully understand why God created us as we are, I have faith enough in my Maker to trust his judgment. We have never "fallen" from perfection. We have never been banned from paradise. We have never been exiled east of Eden.

This interpretation of a blameless human creation generates dilemmas. Much of our religious worldview is built on the supposed bedrock of Adam and Eve and the Fall. How do we handle the issue of original sin if there is no original sin? Certainly sin, evil and suffering are realities in our world. As one of my theology professors, Zachary Hayes, mentions in *What Are They Saying About Creation?*:

> More generally, it can be said that one of the functions of any religious system is to provide a context of meaning within which believers can come to terms with the major questions of human life, among which the problem of pain, suffering, and sin is a major human concern. Indeed, the basic experience which lies behind any religious attempt to deal with sin and evil is the underlying conviction that all is not well with the world.

Thomas Aldworth

So the theological recognition of God's perfection, coupled with the universally human experience of sin and evil, led to the creation of Adam and Eve. Yet no matter how we might seek to explain the origin of evil and sinfulness, I think it's time we pardoned our proto-parents. While we carry our ancestors with us in more ways than just hair color and the shape of our noses, we should finally forgive our mythical first parents and stop using them as an easy answer to a hard question.

Certainly not all the God images that come to us from Scripture are unhealthy or theologically unfit. From the destroying Warrior God found in the earlier books of the Bible, we progress to the Lover God revealed in the writings of some of the prophets. It appears our understanding of God develops as we develop. Or, as the columnist Sydney J. Harris aptly phrased it: "God grows as we grow, for he reflects what we become."

The theology of God's ever-faithful love presented in the Book of Hosea, for instance, is captivating. The prophet Hosea is married to an unfaithful wife, Gomer. Even though Gomer is unfaithful to him, Hosea continually forgives her and takes her back. Hosea sees his own personal situation as analogous to God's relationship with the people Israel. They may often be unfaithful to God but he takes them back again and again.

Fashioning a Healthier Religion

Of course, the God-portrait of Hosea hangs side-by-side with the Warrior God of the Torah. The God who sides with the Israelites in battle is disturbing to many religious people. Of course, the Warrior God is understandable in light of the theology of that time. Recall that the Israelites, for much of the Old Testament, believed there were other gods. It was their God, Yahweh, who was the strongest. It was only natural, then, that the Israelites would be triumphant in battle. A people's god always went before them into combat. When armies clashed, their respective gods also clashed. Since the Israelites believed Yahweh to be the strongest, whenever they lost in battle, they were obviously being punished for some sinful transgression.

The so-called "Promised Land" was split into two kingdoms after the death of Solomon. When the northern kingdom of Israel was conquered by the Assyrians in 712 B.C. and the southern kingdom of Judah was vanquished by the Babylonians in 587 B.C., the Israelites could only believe they were being punished for some form of unfaithfulness. Since God was so powerful, no nation or god could defeat him. The enemies of the Israelites could not be victorious unless God allowed such victories as punishment to them.

This sin-punishment theology so prevalent in the Bible unsettles me. I suspect much of it arose from

Thomas Aldworth

the experience of feeling "chosen." While I believe God "revealed" himself to the Israelites, I struggle with the notion of any people being God's "chosen people." While the people Israel were among the first to recognize themselves as being in a unique relationship with God, that uniqueness shouldn't imply that God doesn't desire a relationship with all peoples. The fact that the Israelites understood themselves as being "chosen" doesn't make everyone else "unchosen." God desires all peoples to be "chosen." If certain people don't feel "chosen," the fault lies with them and not with God. There are no "favorites" in God's family. The relationship which the Israelites had with God is the relationship which all people have with God. God doesn't wander through the world selecting "chosen ones."

While much of our Judaeo-Christian theology is fashioned from God's supposed "election" of the Israelites, I think such "election-theology" does a disservice to God. God was (and is) striving to reveal himself to all his children. The Israelites glimpsed a portion of that revelation. They were able to recognize God as a personal God, a God in relationship with them. Other peoples during Old Testament times were entangled with gods and goddesses with whom a covenant relationship was impossible.

God "revealed" or rather "unveiled" himself throughout the pages of the Old Testament. The people Israel were able to hear the voice of God and respond to it, even though sometimes the voice was barely discernable. The authors of the Old Testament tried to write down what they "heard." The Biblical writers believed God was their God first and foremost. And he was (and is). But because God was (and is) the God of Abraham, Isaac and Jacob doesn't mean that he is not also the God of Confucius, Siddharta and Mohammed. Moses "heard" God's voice better than most of their ancestors. But "hearing" God's voice doesn't make anyone or any people more "chosen" than another. It just means they are graced with good ears.

Being both comforted and confronted by Scripture, I marvel at all its facets. As Rabbi Heschel says: "It (Scripture) continues to scatter seeds of justice and compassion, to echo God's cry to the world and to pierce man's armor of callousness." All of us who share in the Judaeo-Christian tradition have had our world-view immensely influenced by the images and truths of Scripture. We are truly Scriptural people. But being rooted in Scripture doesn't require us to eat everything on the Biblical tree.

Arguably, the most fundamental Biblical belief is that God controls everything. If a storm happens, God wanted it to happen. If a child dies, God wanted that child to die. If a person gets sick, God wanted that person sick. But such a deterministic

Thomas Aldworth

view leads to theological disaster. Did God want (or allow—which is the same thing) the extermination camps of Nazi Germany? Did God want the cities of Hiroshima and Nagasaki to suffer nuclear annihilation? The so-called "silence of God" in view of 20th century horrors is not easily answered, especially if God is in complete control.

I like the image of God presented in Andrew Greeley's novel *The Rite of Spring:*

> (Monsignor Blackie Ryan speaking) "And I don't accept that God is responsible for the tragedy of Ron Crowley and Madonna Clifford. He wanted their stories to be very different, and He was unable to write them the way He wanted. I reject all other explanations."
>
> (Brendan Ryan speaking) "But what does that do to God's omnipotence?"
>
> (Monsignor Ryan) "Omnipotence be damned! . . . Anytime the necessities of Greek philosophy force us into a position that is at odds with the scriptural self-revelation of God, I say reject Greek philosophy. But we have raised generation upon generation of Roman Catholics to believe, not because of the Scriptures, but because of Greek philosophy, that everything that happens in the world is directly attributable to God. That, it seems to me, is patent nonsense . . . God is the great improviser, the great player-by-ear. When bad things happen, or we do bad things

to one another, He simply adjusts His game plan and achieves His goals by an alternative path."

If God is indeed "The Great Improviser," as suggested in *The Rite of Spring*, then we'll have to revise some of our views about salvation history. Our usual understanding of what is called "salvation history" is that God has a plan and everything happens accordingly. It would be spiritually healthier to visualize God revising his plan as the future unfolds.

A God who is continually revising may appear too "situational" for many. Such a God requires more faith than one who knows the future infallibly. It's easier to believe in a God who demands nothing more from us than obedience to his plan. It's difficult to believe in a God who is actively engaged with us in the unfolding of history. We, coupled with God, are responsible for achieving the plan which God has in his mind and heart. As Francis J. Smith points out in *The God Question: A Catholic Approach:*

> God does not take away from us our responsibility for history. . . . God gives us courage to act in history because God wants to achieve our salvation within history through our acceptance of our responsibility for history.

If everything has already been "ordained" then no genuine freedom exists. People who hold to God's absolute control, that everything which happens does so because he wills it, get caught in a kind of despair. Belief in God's foreknowledge, that God knows everything which will happen, leads to fatalism. Faith and fatalism make unhealthy allies. While God has an infinitely better idea about what will happen in the future than I do, there still must be times when God himself is surprised. Without such potential for surprise, we could not become loving people. God has, in a sense, given up absolute control so we might have the freedom we need to chose loving behavior.

Many people, for instance, believe that the day of their death is written down in some sort of heavenly ledger. They may even exploit such a belief to justify their own foolish life choices. "Well, it doesn't matter if I smoke or not—when it's your time, it's your time!" I don't accept that the day of my death is written down anywhere, even in the heart of God. It may well be that "all the hairs of my head are numbered" but the present number of my head hairs and the date of my death are unrelated. One has to do with the present. The other with the future. I believe the future to be obscure, opaque, even to God. He knows all that is knowable but the future remains unknowable. God cannot know everything about the future if there exists authentic free will and human freedom.

This issue of God's foreknowledge drags me into

admittedly deep waters. Being a poor swimmer, I admit some hesitancy. This hesitancy reminds me of the first, and so far only, time I jumped off a diving board. As I mentioned in *Shaping A Healthy Religion,* I had never learned to swim as a child. The only swimming pool in our neighborhood was at the local YMCA. We Catholics were warned about going there to swim. I suspected that Protestant children secreted something into the water that would make us lose our faith. And so it wasn't until college that I had the chance to learn the intricacies of swimming.

After a few months of paddling around in our college seminary pool, I began to feel cocky. I felt I'd mastered the nuances of swimming. I decided to test my neonate mastery by jumping off the diving board. My classmates assured me there was nothing to it. I would go down to the bottom of the pool and then push myself back up. Coming to the surface, I would easily swim to the side of the pool. Or so I was led to believe. But when I jumped off the board, I didn't go down to the bottom nor did I come back to the surface. I wound up in the middle of the deep end, neither sinking nor rising! Experiencing some alarm, I stretched out my hand, breaking the surface of the water. Making a motion with my hand, I tried to indicate that I was in the process of drowning. A classmate, who currently operates a

Thomas Aldworth

funeral home in Indianapolis, saw my plight, jumped in and pulled me to safety. I haven't jumped off a diving board since. I freely admit strong feelings of self-preservation!

When it comes to theological speculation, many of us have analogous self-preservation feelings. What if we get it wrong? What if we make a mistake in judging who God is? Won't God somehow want to "get us" for our mistake? I believe God is more tolerant than we suspect. Since he made us as we are, with a hunger for understanding, God probably enjoys our religious speculations. In some ways, coming to God is like jumping off a diving board. Sometimes we have to risk the jump. In other ways, coming to God is like going on a blind date. We've been told by others how great God is but we still experience hesitation. How many times have blind dates really turned out well? I don't know the answer since I've never been on a blind date but I suspect God may be the ultimate blind date.

We need to be careful about those who want to get in the way of our coming to God. These people claim to know without doubt who God is and what God is doing. They remind me of the chaperons who were part and parcel of dating in the olden days. I suspect it was difficult to get to know one's date when there was a flock of chaperons fluttering about. I see many self-declared "religious" people clamoring to be chaperons on our God-date. They thwart any possible intimacy between God and us.

This intimacy is even more difficult because of the distorted "descriptions" of God that we've been given. If our image of God relies mainly on early Scripture "descriptions," then we won't be able to "see" God even when we're "looking" straight at him. If we depend primarily on other people's depictions of God, then we won't be able to follow the portrait painted on the canvas of our own heart.

If we don't try to refine the God images we've been given, we'll wind up looking for God in all the wrong places, to paraphrase the old country/western song. We need to search for God with the openness and emptiness which comes from discarding the excess baggage of shallow God views. But such "discarding" is painful. We may have to toss out things to which we've become attached. Achieving an "emptiness" for God is a most demanding process. Many of us are so internally littered with God-expectations and God-descriptions that there's no room for God within. I've known a number of people who found it impossible to throw anything out. Their homes were crammed from floor to ceiling with junk. I'm not sure what psychological factor was at work in such people but I do know many of us are crammed internally from floor to ceiling.

Part of our difficulty revolves around the language

we use to call God's name in our search for him. How do we name God? In the past we usually fashioned God in masculine patriarchal terms. I realize the turmoil this has caused many believers, especially women. To think of God only as a male does a disservice to God and to us. God is both male and female—as well as neither male or female (a bit of a conundrum). Yet sexual imagery has a definite place when it comes to talking about what God does. God indeed "fathers" us, but he also "mothers" us. He "sisters" us as well as "brothers" us. God is best fathomed by using both masculine and feminine analogies.

God language serves no purpose unless it helps us experience God. If thinking and talking of God in purely masculine terms doesn't help us come to God, then we need to think and talk about God in terms which will. But we would well remember that our mystical tradition teaches us that in relationship to God, we are all feminine. In much of our mystical tradition, the soul is perceived as being feminine. God and the soul become joined in decidedly masculine/feminine symbolism. The marital union of man and woman is understood as the ultimate analogy of how God and our soul are united. As Jeremiah 20:7 makes clear, God "seduces" us. Such seduction abides at the core of all true spirituality.

Perhaps we can visualize God as having a masculine and a feminine side, just as people have a masculine and feminine side. In the terminology of the Swiss psychoanalyst Carl Jung, everyone has an "animus" or masculine side and an "anima" or feminine side. Wholeness has to do with allowing both the animus and the anima to develop. We certainly focused too strongly in the past on the "animus" of God. But to deny the animus altogether would not help correct the imbalance. Both aspects of God's "personality" need to be theologically developed. God must be both/and—a perpetual paradox.

I do use masculine pronouns when I speak of God. I use the term "Father" often in liturgies. I've been accused of chauvinism because of such masculine terminology. While I may be a chauvinist, I find the neuterless name "God" to be dull. I prefer to get personal. I suspect God also likes to get personal. As George Montague notes in *Our Father, Our Mother:* "It should, of course, be obvious that replacing 'Father' with a neuter title depersonalizes God and makes intimacy impossible." God forbid that God and intimacy not be eternally fused together! God is either about relationships or Nietzsche was right in claiming God to be dead.

I'm a bit of a romantic at heart. I'm not sure if that's a blessing or a curse. Probably a combination of both. But I find myself caught in some sort of

Thomas Aldworth

celestial romance. I've become a trifle "smitten." I'm not sure if I'm the suitor or the sought. I'm not certain if I'm "chasing" or being "chased." One thing I am sure of, however, is that I welcome this divine courtship.

CHAPTER TWO

Salvation

FROM earliest childhood, I worried about salvation, particularly my own. All church ritual seemed to exist for the sole purpose of getting me and my fellow believers to heaven. The Sisters who taught us at Saint Leo grade school implied we had to "earn" our way into heaven. Since Adam and Eve had messed things up in the beginning, we'd have to spend our lives earning heaven by doing good and avoiding evil.

Many of us continue to get caught in a salvation-fixation. I've been asked many times, usually by total strangers, if I've been saved. This question was more likely during the eight years I lived in the "Bible Belt" of northern Louisiana, but I've even been asked the question in the urban setting of Cleveland. While usually answering in the affirmative, I've been known to offer a more belligerent response depending upon mood. I find it offensive to go about the world shouting "I've been saved." Such shouting strikes me as a twisted form of pride. That's especially true if the one "saved" proclaims what a wretched sinner he or she was before being "saved." While I have nothing against being converted and changing one's life, I become uncomfortable when people chant their past sins with so much relish.

What is salvation all about anyway? What are we being saved from and saved for? To understand let's look at what is known as "salvation history." Salvation history is generally understood as the history of God's activity in our world. But, as noted earlier, I have difficulty with the traditional starting point of salvation history—the Fall of Adam and Eve from Eden. Humanity has never walked in paradise. While humans may have broken a kind of instinctual innocence with their evolutionary arrival, suggestions of a fall from a mythical "magic kingdom" belong in the realm of fairy tales, not history. As Dick Westley notes in *Redemptive Intimacy:* "By now almost all of us Christians agree that the Book of Genesis account of creation is not to be taken as literally true."

If we continue to have the fall of our first ancestors as the starting point of our salvation theology, we will not be able to understand what God might be doing in our world. We'll be incapable of perceiving what God might be doing because we assume he's still dealing with the after-effects of "apple-eating." We'll continue living our lives with a chip on our shoulders, feeling unjustly oppressed because of a primordial disobedience. We'll wander through life with an Adam-Eve attitude problem, feeling disgruntled by what we believe happened at the dawn of our human race.

Our usual understanding of salvation history is also rather selfishly distorted. We claim the pivotal point of creation to be the planet earth. We've been led (or misled) to believe that God created the entire universe just so we would have life. If that's true, then God is wildly exorbitant in his creative activity. What would be the point of the expanse of the cosmos? Why, if the earth is the focus of creation, would we be some 30,000 light years from the center of our own galaxy? Why create a universe some 16 or so billion light years across? Maybe God just got carried away? As Zachary Hayes points out in *What Are They Saying About Creation?*:

> We may well be astonished and overawed by the immensity of the universe as seen through the eyes of science. It may be difficult to imagine that an intelligent God would act in such an extravagant and uneconomical manner. If the stellar systems were intended only to produce a planet capable of life, would an intelligent God have employed such a vast machinery for this purpose?

Almost all our theology was fashioned with a different understanding of the universe, a different cosmology, in mind. It's only been in contemporary times that we've begun to comprehend the vastness of space. Until recently the sun and stars were thought

Thomas Aldworth

to be relatively close to the earth. Only in this century has our vision exploded. As Neil McAleer notes in *The Cosmic Mind-Boggling Book:* "In just 15 years (1917-32), the size of the known universe expanded 1 trillion times." We've come to know that our sun is only one of a possible 200 billion stars in our own galaxy. We've discovered our Milky Way Galaxy to be only one of an estimated 100 billion galaxies, each with their own billions of stars! We've also ascertained, according to McAleer, that our galaxy is flying through the universe at about 1.4 million miles per hour, heading in the direction of the constellation Hydra. It's a wild ride we're on! We've definitely lost the simple, solid world-view of the ancients.

And yet while our view of the universe has furiously unfolded, our theology remains relatively earth-bound. If life is ever found on other planets, what will that do to our theology? Will each planet with life have to develop its own salvation history? I personally hope there's life elsewhere besides earth. Yet many of us may want to believe the universe exists only for us. God must love us so much that he couldn't possibly have any love left over for other worlds or other creatures.

Part of our hesitancy about God loving other worlds may have to do with the distances involved in cosmic travel. Do we really believe God can be here in our piece of galactic space and also at the far edge of our galaxy, some 100,000 light years away, with a light year being roughly 9.5 thousand billion kilometers? Can God be watching over the earth while simultaneously keeping a similar vigil in a far-distant galaxy? It seems simpler to just say we're the only living things and be done with such speculation.

But good theology must take into account what is. We cannot avoid the vastness of our universe. Such vastness must affect our understanding of God and our understanding of salvation. I hope for an astronomer-theologian who will help us understand what we might wish to believe as we gaze into the night sky. If our theologians don't develop a spirituality pertinent to our space age, then Hollywood will do it for us. And may the Force then be with us!

I also struggle with salvation being usually limited to humans. As Zachary Hayes notes in *Visions of a Future—A Study of Christian Eschatology:* "Only unmitigated pride and conceit would allow us to say that God is concerned only with the human race and that questions about the rest of creation are of no religious or theological relevance." I appreciate the statement near the end of the 4th Eucharistic Prayer which proclaims: "Then, in your kingdom, freed from the corruption of sin and death, *we shall sing your glory with every creature* through Christ our Lord." Such an assertion suggests that salvation won't be limited to human life. All life will somehow share in salvation. All

Thomas Aldworth

creatures will sing God's glory together. When I'm asked by children if their dead dog is in heaven, I have no hesitation in assuring them their dog is indeed with God.

Now this gets complicated. If God takes dead dogs to himself, what about dead cockroaches and dead sharks? Will fire ants share in eternal glory? Will the two million known species of creatures all pass through the "pearly gates"? How does this affect extinct species? Will Tyrannosaurs Rex be prowling heaven's corridors? Will smallpox be wafting through the celestial air? I admit being in trouble here but I don't see how heaven could be heaven without a myriad of creatures. I admittedly don't know how this might work out in practice.

Since the evangelist John, we Christians have spoken of the coming of "a new heaven and a new earth." Our Christian view of the end of things is intimately tied to the re-creation of the earth. We're not intended to spend eternity in heaven. We're meant to spend eternity on a new earth. How this "new earth" is to be made a reality is a mystery to me but it's certainly our Christian expectation. Again turning to Hayes:

> These (metaphors of a new heaven and a new earth) are not only a biblical language for a hoped-for future. Indeed, they are the language of the human heart itself

Fashioning a Healthier Religion

as it struggles to find a home for itself in a world that seems hostile to its efforts. The word that God addresses to us through history is directed to the deepest roots of our human nature and opens to human hope the prospect of an absolute future in which all the good, the true, and the beautiful brought forth in history is brought to fulfillment and crowned with eternal significance in the life of God . . . the Christian hopes for an absolute fulfillment of created existence without knowing precisely how this will be brought about or what it will be like. (From *Visions of a Future: A Study of Christian Eschatology*)

Being Franciscan, I have a historical weakness for creatures. I've always tried to have a blessing of the animals wherever I've found myself in ministry. Usually this "pet blessing" is celebrated in conjunction with the feast of Francis of Assisi on October 4th. These animal blessings have been a source of great joy to me over the years. They've also been a "mixed" blessing at times.

I remember one of the pet blessings from my years as campus minister at Louisiana Tech University in Ruston, Louisiana. A friend of mine brought her three dogs to be blessed. She'd recently "adopted" a large male stray, who had a lot of Irish wolfhound in him. This dog, named "Funny", was very friendly to people and to the two female dogs he lived with. Little did we suspect how he'd react to other male dogs!

43

Thomas Aldworth

Just as we began the blessing, I heard a horrible commotion and looked over to see Funny with a small dog in his mouth, shaking the poor creature up and down like a rag doll. After retrieving the critter, we tied Funny to a tree, hoping to prevent any further incident. He managed to free himself, however, and was soon chomping on another dog, at which point when he was "banished" from the blessing. It's embarrassing having such excitement at a parish pet blessing, especially since a reporter from the local paper was taking pictures!

My first pet blessing in Grambling, Louisiana, where I spent four years as pastor and campus minister, was also exciting. One of the lovely elders of the parish brought her female pit bull "Lady Di" to be blessed. Lady Di first tried to mount a surprised male dog. Then she got loose and took off down the street. Since her owner was unable to move quickly because of age and arthritis, the task of retrieving Lady Di fell to me. So off I went, in full Franciscan habit, on the trail of the runaway hound. There were many Grambling State University students on the streets. I'm not sure what entered their minds as they saw me running down the street in my habit, chasing this furry fugitive.

I also recall blessing a grumpy dog named "Frosty" during my time in Grambling. I like to place my hand on anything I bless. So Frosty's owner and I both had

Fashioning a Healthier Religion

our hands on his head. I could feel the little beast growling beneath my palm. After the blessing, I began to take my hand away but his owner took her hand away a split second before mine. That was all the time Frosty needed. Latching onto two of my fingers, he chewed on them until I yanked them from his mouth. I realized a Franciscan habit isn't all the protection it could be. Or maybe Frosty just hadn't heard about Francis and the wolf of Gubbio?

Dog tales aside, we do need to encourage our theologians to continue wrestling with the dynamics of salvation. The ecological dimensions of religion need to be pondered. Otherwise I fear our children may have to choose between traditional religious concepts and the contemporary hodgepodge known as "New Age." There needs to be a middle ground that helps us appreciate biblical faith without becoming fundamentalistically rigid. The question of salvation may be the crucible for creating this needed middle ground.

A broader understanding of salvation than normally proclaimed from our pulpits would be helpful. For a long time, we've limited salvation. We've conditioned it. Only Catholics would be saved. Only Christians would be saved. Only church-goers would be saved. Only believers in this or that would be saved. We continue placing conditions on what seems to be a freely-given gift from God.

Obviously, I don't know who will be saved. I

wouldn't want to suggest that everyone will find salvation. With our freedom, we must be able to choose to shun salvation if we want to. But I suspect salvation will be broader than I was led to believe in grade school. I'm sure there will be more than the 144,000 suggested in the Book of Revelations.

Speaking of the 144,000 reminds me of an experience I had while training in clinical pastoral education at Baptist Memorial Hospital in San Antonio. One of the tasks we had as chaplains was to talk with the families of those who died at the hospital. One day I found myself summoned to the room of a woman who had just expired. When I got there, I met the dead woman's daughter. After bringing her to a waiting room, the first thing she demanded of me was "Are you one of the 144,000 who will be saved?" I was dumbstruck. I suggested we might want to talk about her mother. She continued to ask me if I was one of the 144,000.

Not really wanting to debate John's theology, I told her I believed there would be more than 144,000 saved. I pointed out that the number 144,000 was meant to be an unlimited number and how John talk also about "a huge crowd which no one could count from every nation and race, people and tongue." But the woman didn't want to listen. Her mother's death seemed less important to her than finding out if I was

Fashioning a Healthier Religion

among the 144,000. It's possible the daughter was suffering a hysterical reaction to her mother's death but I quickly excused myself and escaped the encounter.

Another place where the battle of salvation is fought is the area of evolution. By now most people accept some form of evolution, even though fundamentalists often demand Creationism be taught as a legitimate alternate. It seems logical that human life took some time to emerge. I get headaches from Creationists who insist the devil planted fossils in the earth to confuse us and make us susceptible to the "devilish" theory of evolution. While Creationists are sincere in trying to reconcile the view of creation found in Genesis with current scientific ideology, they erroneously pit religion against science.

Let's take a look at the scenario of creation as currently viewed by science. Some billions of years ago, a star exploded in our region of space. The "debris" from that supernova explosion condensed to form our present sun and the planets which comprise our solar system. Our earth was formed between four and five billion years ago. We know the earth could not have been created in what is described as the "big bang" since only hydrogen and helium were produced in that primal outburst. All other elements, such as carbon, the basis of life, were baked in stars and released in the blasts of supernovae. If a star had not exploded

Thomas Aldworth

in our corner of the cosmos, there could not have been any earth or, obviously, earthly life. Stars are the instruments of life, the clay in the potter's hands.

Our earth, reportedly, is roughly four billion years old, which is interesting in view of our approximately 16 billion year old universe. God, who I believe to be the author of creation, waited almost 12 billion years before creating our planet. And though our earth is four billion years old, life didn't begin until about two billion years ago. That primitive life began in the oceans. Some form of life crawled unto land 400 million years ago. The great age of the dinosaurs followed. Human life, in terms of homo sapiens, began about 250,000 years ago. Homo sapiens sapiens, the sub-species to which we belong, didn't become reality until 50,000 years ago.

The reason for this quick dash through time is to point out how egotistical we can be concerning what God may or may not be doing in creation. We assume God created the cosmos just for our tiny world whirling through space. We presume God began our planetary process just so human life could evolve. While that may be the case, God certainly took his time about it. It might be better to agree with Zachary Hayes' *What Are They Saying About Creation?* when he asserts:"There is no reason to assume the mere fact of human life is the goal of the universe."

When I read about the suspected progression of life

Fashioning a Healthier Religion

on earth, I'm amazed human life developed at all. Remember that dinosaurs ruled our world for 150 million years. Large mammals could not have evolved unless the dinosaurs were exterminated. That's precisely what happened about 65 million years ago. Without that extinction, we wouldn't be here. Did God "cause" the extinction of the dinosaurs? I don't think so, which leads me to suspect that human life is not the sole purpose of evolution.

Contemporary research, such as presented in Stephen Jay Gould's *Wonderful Life—The Burgess Shale and the Nature of History*, suggests a rather haphazard evolutionary process. There have been many "dead ends." A randomness appears inherent in evolution. And yet here we are! So we need to thank God, whom I heartily believe to be the source of creation and the force behind evolution. I don't think we're the final product. I believe we'll continue unfolding into the fullness of humanness and life awaiting us in God's mind.

In view of the vastness of the universe, we need a vision of God corresponding to such vastness. Looking at God is like looking at the ocean. I've a special fondness for ocean views. I wrote *Shaping a Healthy Religion* on the Hawaiian island of Maui. I returned there to write this book. As I would gaze out across the ocean, I saw only the ocean's surface. I couldn't see the great depth or breadth of it. I couldn't see the immense quantity of life contained in it. As I eyed the ocean, I could glimpse only a sliver of it. There was no way to comprehend its fullness.

God is like the ocean. We catch only a glimpse of the "surface" of God. We can't "see" God's fullness. Yet no connection like people who think they understand the ocean because they have seen its surface, so there are many who claim to know God because they have seen God's "surface." They proclaim who God is and what God wants even though they've only put their toe into the "ocean" of God or waded into God up to their knees.

I'm fearful of the ocean. My fearfulness arises from a combination of poor swimming ability, coupled with a primordial wariness of the myriad of hungry, ocean-creatures. Those of us who have seen "Jaws" will always harbor a touch of paranoia when we wade into the ocean. I remember being on a beach in Michigan City, Indiana around the time "Jaws" debuted. I overheard a child expressing qualms about venturing into Lake Michigan because of "Jaws." I assured him sharks didn't inhabit the fresh water of the Great Lakes.

Just as I'm fearful of the ocean, so I'm fearful of God. I suspect such fearfulness is common in those of us who were given a "traditional" Catholic upbringing. We're always waiting for God to somehow "get us." We look at the surface of God and hear the

Fashioning a Healthier Religion

"Jaws" theme. It's no wonder, then, that many of us flee from belief in God when we get the chance. We've been taught to fear God so much that we run away when the opportunity arises. Of course, escape from God isn't possible, as Abraham Heschel reminds us:

> We can sever ourselves from the dimension of the holy neither by sin nor by stupidity, neither by apostasy nor by ignorance . . . There is no escape from God.

Part of the process for transforming our fear involves appreciating the purpose of eternity. We've been promised an everlasting mystical union. In our mystical union with God, all barriers will be broken down. Full acceptance will happen. Just as in a marriage where both partners are truly open to each other, so in the mystical union, there will be little to fear. Complete openness and acceptance will allow us to finally surrender our defenses. We'll spend forever united with God in a union similar to one possible between two fully loving people. God's love will indeed cast out all fear. I joyfully anticipate swimming fearlessly in the eternal ocean of God.

Of course, many of us may not want to spend eternity united with God. We haven't learned how attractive we are to God and how attractive he can be to us. As Alan Jones notes in *Soul Making:* "God is the One who attracts, lures, draws us to himself." God is eminently seductive—a "femme fatale" or

Thomas Aldworth

"hunk" depending upon the metaphors we use. As Edwin Clark Johnson reminds us in his *In Search of God in the Sexual Underworld: A Mystical Journey:* "It is God's beauty which is at the base of sexual attractiveness." The beauty we see in each other is intimately linked with the beauty of God. The sexual "stirring" we engender in each other has a divine origin.

Wouldn't our adolescence have been more tolerable if we'd been told that sexual attraction wasn't so much a temptation as a manifestation of our Creator? So many of us were given images of a disappointed and disapproving God as we tramped through the booby-trapped terrain of puberty. How could we understand the seductiveness of salvation when we were given distorted notions of sexuality?

I certainly received sexual distortions in the minor seminary, which I had entered at the tender and terrible age of thirteen. The seminary, which closed some years ago, was in one of the Chicago suburbs. My twin brother, Jack, went to the seminary with me. It seemed a glorious adventure. But I soon began to see that something was amiss. Our librarian would censor every magazine before putting them out for us to read. Any picture with the faint possibility of arousing our adolescent hearts was summarily cut from the magazine. Since it was a boarding seminary, we rarely saw any females, especially the younger variety. It is not surprising that many of us prowled around on the monthly "Visiting Sunday," peering at and, perhaps, timidly leering at our classmates' sisters.

In the seminary we were given the impression our sexual stirrings were offensive to God. While almost all Catholics were warned about the "sins of the flesh," we seminarians were given a lethal dose of sexual guilt. Each morning, as we waited for mass to begin, a number of us would line up at the confessional. It was rightly suspected that most of those in line were there because they had "fallen into sin" the previous night either through thoughts or touches. We had to suppress all sexual imaginings and cravings if we were to be "holy" enough for communion.

It would have helped us retain some sexual sanity if we'd been taught that sexuality was not the result of sin but rather how God designed us to continue our species. As Edwin C. Johnson notes: "Our sexuality, far from being a distraction from God, can be understood as the instrument by which God created us and continues to manifest himself to us."

Many turn from our church because of our sexual ethics. We've given the impression to most of our people that the question of salvation rotates around how we handle sexuality. While I'll talk more about that later, right now I'd like to suggest one of the reasons why we have a distorted salvation/sexuality theology. My suggestion returns us to the Adam and Eve story. As the early church struggled to understand the question of redemption/salvation, they focused on the sin of Adam and Eve.

James A. Brundage notes in *Law, Sex, and Christian Society in Medieval Europe:*

> The great Biblical exegete, Origen (ca. A.D. 185-253), and the anonymous author of the Gnostic *Gospel according to the Egyptians,* for example, believed that Adam and Eve had been innocent of sexual temptations or even sexual feelings in Paradise. When they committed the first sin by disobeying God's command not to eat of the fruit of the tree of knowledge, Adam and Eve introduced sex into the world and with it the evil of death. With sex came death.

While the Gnostics were recognized as heretical, they had quite an impact on the theology of the early church. Even those who were not Gnostic fell under the sway of believing the Fall altered sexuality. As Brundage continues:

> According to Augustine, Adam and Eve had known sex in Paradise, although it was a different kind of sex from the sort we experience, for the very physiology of reproduction changed as a result of sin. Prior to the Fall the sexual organs had been under conscious control; but just as our first parents rebelled against God, so after the Fall our genitals rebelled

against our will. Humans then became incapable of controlling either their sexual desires or the physical reactions of their gonads.

What I'm suggesting with these readings is that we've had a distorted understanding of sexuality for a long time. Certainly Augustine has had a profound impact on Christian theology. As Elaine Pagels tells us in her fascinating *Adam, Eve, and the Serpent:* "From the fifth century on, Augustine's pessimistic views of sexuality, politics, and human nature would become the dominant influence on western Christianity, both Catholic and Protestant, and color all western culture, Christian or not, ever since."

Understanding Adam and Eve's Fall as resulting in an altering of our sexual physiology, Augustine obviously saw human sexuality/reproduction as a "fallen" or "soiled" process. He assumed God really didn't intend for us to propagate the way we do. Before the Fall, we had no lustful thoughts. We were different than we are. Adam and Eve's disobedience re-wired our circuits.

Yet, contrary to Augustine, I believe we're the way we are because God wished us to be this way. We were never more "perfect" than we are now. While I recognize the reality of sin and our human history of sinfulness, I can't accept that we've ever been significantly different than we are at present. Perhaps it's time to accept our creation for what it

Thomas Aldworth

is — a gift and grace from our Creator. Our first
parents are not to blame for our human imperfections or the imperfections of our world. I realize
questions then arise concerning original sin. I don't
believe we're born with the residue of Adam and
Eve's sin but perhaps we're born as reluctant heirs
to our whole history of human sinfulness.

If we're basically the way God intended us to be,
then we'll have to understand salvation history differently concerning the coming of Jesus. When Jesus
comes among us as the son of the Father, he doesn't
so much reverse the sin of Adam and Eve as confront the sinfulness of the human condition. Salvation is the journey from the slavery of sin to the
freedom of the Father. Jesus shows us how to make
that journey.

We can continue understanding Jesus saving us
from sin even if we discount the sin of Adam and
Eve. Because of our humanity, we will continue to
fail and fall. We'll continue to sin not because of an
original sin but because of our God-designed human
nature. Sin exists because of free will. If we were
unable to sin, we'd also be unable to love. Love, as
well as sin, demands free will. Sin, then, is the
"shadow" side of loving. And it is love which is the
salvific task. Salvation has as much to do with love
as with sin. Since sin happens when we refuse to
love, salvation happens when we choose to love.

Fashioning a Healthier Religion

Our lifelong conversion must be a lifetime pursuit of increased mastery of loving. Jesus shows us how to achieve this mastery through his death-embracing trust in the Father's love.

Salvation must involve coming to know the Father's love. Because of the God images I was given, I spent many years wondering if God really loved me. I figured God would love me only if I was good, only if I obeyed my parents, only if I did well in school, only if I didn't fight with my brothers. It has taken me a long time to realize God loves me no matter what I do. If I stumble into sin, or even brazenly embrace it, God still loves me. While sin makes me incapable of experiencing the Father's love by keeping me unaware of it, it doesn't alter the love which God has for me. Sin doesn't prevent God's love. Sin doesn't make God want to punish me or "get even."

All religions proclaim the love of God but often with strings attached. God will love you only if you follow all the proscriptions of the Torah, as proclaimed by Leviticus 20:22: "Be careful to observe all my statutes and all my decrees; otherwise the land where I am bringing you to dwell will vomit you out." That sounds like conditional love! Or God will love you only if you are faithful to the Koran. Or God will love you only if you follow the Gospels. Or God will love you only if you do this or that.

Thomas Aldworth

Strings keep getting attached to what God wishes to freely give.

The saving experience of God is not the experience of obeying a multitude of Biblical laws and decrees. Those of us who are Christian have long ago stopped obeying the laws laid out in books such as Leviticus and Deuteronomy. Why we don't even obey the third commandment. We've never kept the sabbath holy. The sabbath is from sunset Friday until sunset Saturday. Sunday is not the sabbath nor has it ever been the sabbath. We Christians "break" the third commandment weekly.

From 1986 until 1990, I was the pastor of Saint Benedict the Black in Grambling, Louisiana. The parish exists primarily to serve the students at Grambling State University, a predominately black university. Many of the people in the parish share ancestral memories of slavery. When we sang songs of freedom, a spirit stirred which knew the cost of freedom.

Many of us Catholics still need freedom. We've been enslaved by false images of God and erroneous notions of salvation. Instead of seeking the face of our Father, we cower and hide from the God who resembles the "bogeyman" of our bad dreams. We are chained with oppressive guilt and unhealthy shame. We still believe we're sinners in the hands of an angry God.

58

Fashioning a Healthier Religion

I'm not suggesting the experience of God is all sweetness and light. God can be like a hurricane. I remember Hurricane Ewa which hit the Hawaiian islands in November, 1982. There was considerable damage to the island of Kaui and the west side of Oahu. Maui was struck by the edge of Ewa. I vividly recall the wind and waves generated by the hurricane. Sitting on what little was left of my favorite beach, I imagined God must act in a similar way, uprooting whatever stands in the way of his powerful presence.

God may indeed be Francis Thompson's immortal "Hound of Heaven." Many of us suffer Thompson's "titanic glooms of chasmed fears" as we flee the God we have been led to misperceive. We flee him "down the nights and down the days." We'd do well to let the heavenly hound finally catch us and bite us on our backside. But we fear such a bite, believing the hound has rabies. We keep God at a distance with our Biblical horror stories.

Perhaps we need to no longer ask "What are we being saved from?" but "What are we being drawn to?" Perhaps the story of Adam and Eve in paradise is not descriptive of what was but rather what will be. Such was the suggestion of Zachary Hayes as we chatted one day over lunch. He said the Adam and Eve story evolved as a post-Exilic dream, a hope of what will be when God's kingdom is complete.

Thomas Aldworth

While I still see the story as fundamentally unhealthy, it may have a slight redemptive value as a vision of where we are heading—a suggestion of the intimacy with God which awaits the completion of salvation history. I, for one, impatiently wait.

CHAPTER THREE

Faith-Fears and Sin

G ROWING up in an Irish Catholic neighborhood on Chicago's Southside, we found religion and life to be intimately connected. Religion was a profound part of our life. Which school my brothers and I would attend was taken for granted. We'd attend the parochial grade school, even though there was a public school less than a block from our house. As we walked past the public school on our way to Saint Leo's, we always felt a touch of smugness. Being Catholic was difficult but in a strange way that made us happy. God obviously expected more of us than he did our Protestant neighbors.

My father was a staunch believer. He attended mass almost every day of his adult life. He loaded freight cars for the Baltimore and Ohio Railroad. It was hard work but he didn't have many options. He hadn't been able to finish much school in his native Ireland. His life was a punishing one. He died when my twin brother and I were eleven. He hadn't been able to give us much in terms of material things but he'd given us an uncompromising regard for religion.

Thomas Aldworth

I remember all the evenings my father would gather us together to say the rosary. I dreaded those times, mostly because my knees weren't fond of kneeling. It also meant the end of any program we might be watching on television. But one did not argue with my father. When he declared "rosary time," it was rosary time. Such an approach, however, didn't leave me with a love for the rosary.

The Sisters of Providence taught me every year I was in grade school. The first teacher I had who wasn't a member of a religious community was my shorthand teacher, Mrs. Flaherty, my senior year of high school. So my world-view was constructed in a decidedly Catholic fashion. While some mistakes got mingled into that world-view, there was no doubt that God was at its core.

The main difficulty I see with the world-view I was given is that it seemed to be based more on fear than faith. Our approach to God was similar to how we approached our pastor. Our pastor was one of those monsignors who seemingly controlled the Irish Southside. Monsignor P.J. Molloy was undoubtedly a good man but those of us who were children had a hard time seeing the goodness. Actually, we tried to avoid Monsignor Molloy. We were terrified of him.

Those of us who were altar boys were especially afraid. Whenever we came to church to serve mass, we'd pray the celebrant would be one of the young

Fashioning a Healthier Religion

assistant pastors, who were usually friendly. We'd breathe a sigh of relief if we saw an assistant coming into the sacristy. But if Monsignor Molloy came in, we'd start to quiver. The monsignor was a rather grumpy celebrant. If one of his servers did anything wrong, the monsignor might well yell at him in front of the entire assembly. He'd been known to even hit a server for a serious Rubrical error. We served his Rubrical masses in mortal fear of doing anything wrong.

We probably respected our pastor but that respect had a strong component of fear. I remember the fear we felt when it came time for our report cards. Report cards at St. Leo's were always given out by one of the parish priests. The priest would call a name and then look at the grades for that student. He would say something like "well done" or "you can do better." The potential for humiliation was significant. This was especially true if the pastor was passing out the report cards. Monsignor Molloy created a flock of over-achievers.

Since our monsignor seemed to be God's right hand man, we children assumed God must be rather like him in personality. God must also be grumpy if he chose this grumpy fellow to pastor us. Or so went our childish logic. Our parochial world was strewn with occasionally grumpy grace.

When I went to the minor seminary, I continued

to encounter grumpy grace. The priests and brothers at the minor seminary were friendly enough but we still lived in fear of them. They had the power to expel us from the seminary, which we believed would make us a traitor to God. We were constantly told in the high school seminary that we'd been "given" a religious vocation and that it was up to us to protect it. If we had a true vocation and didn't accept it, then our lives would be a mess at best.

So, for four long years, my classmates and I endured many little abuses. Out-going mail was turned in unsealed so it could be read. In-coming mail was read before we received it. Our magazines were censored. All the books we brought with us from home had to be approved before we could read them. We slept in large dormitories with a hundred of us laid out barracks-style. We were allowed one television program a week—the Walt Disney Show. We could buy three candy bars a week, one of which was expected to be "donated" to the missions. We kept "the grand silence" from night prayers until breakfast each morning. We studied many long hours and played sports every afternoon. It was a significantly disciplined life. I was considerably unhappy with it.

In addition to the grade school fear we had of God, another element of fear was added by our seminary professors. Along with fearing God, we would now also have to fear females. They could cause us to lose our vocation which would certainly weaken our chances for salvation. And seeking salvation is what brought many of us to the seminary in the first place. Becoming a priest seemed the shortest and surest route to salvation. No telling when God might have an attack of "the grumps" and start tossing people into hell. We figured priests would naturally be on God's "good side." No use taking chances with hell-fire!

I remember the talk given by the seminary rector prior to our first Christmas vacation. We were all clustered in the chapel, anxiously awaiting this first opportunity to return home. The rector began by telling us how careful we'd need to be during our time away from the "protection" of the seminary. We were no longer just ordinary fellows. We were seminarians. People expected a higher level of conduct from us. We'd be under the constant scrutiny of those searching for flaws in our character. This was especially true when it came to our conduct with girls. Everyone in our neighborhood would know we were "chosen." We could give serious scandal if we didn't have a "holy" demeanor in our associations with girls. Girls could make us refuse the call we had received and surely God wouldn't overlook such a refusal.

Walking home from the grocery store one day during that Christmas vacation, I bumped into Margaret Stevens, who I had taken to my first dance. She

Thomas Aldworth

wanted to know how I was doing and what the seminary was like. My heart felt like it would break out of my chest. Here was someone who could keep me from doing God's will! I stammered a few words and then fled from her as if she were sin incarnate. She must have thought the seminary created lunatics. Because my family moved soon afterward, I never saw Margaret again. I've always wanted to apologize for fleeing from her that Christmas-time, 1961. Back in the safety of the seminary, I realized I was no longer just afraid of God. I now feared any human love which could keep me from accepting my "sacred" call. It hadn't occurred to me yet that love was exactly God's sacred call to all.

After graduating from the high school seminary, I went on to the college seminary in Quincy, Illinois. My twin brother left the seminary, got a job with Amoco and wound up in Vietnam. By now I'd lost most of my fear of seminary professors. I became a rebellious sort, a belated beatnik, reading authors I wasn't supposed to read. I became a collegiate cynic, sullenly puffing on Lucky Strikes. I majored for a time in English but decided to switch my major to Drama at the beginning of my junior year. The Academic Dean, however, told me I couldn't switch to Drama. I inquired why. He said I might have to be in a play where I'd kiss a girl on stage. I started to laugh, thinking this was some enigmatic joke. But he assured me

Fashioning a Healthier Religion

it wasn't. Since I was now a Franciscan, having completed my novitiate between my sophomore and junior years, I couldn't take the chance of causing scandal. I tried assuring the dean that I'd never be cast as a hero-type but it was a lost cause. I wound up majoring in Philosophy, concentrating on the French Existentialists.

I remained relatively rebellious during my junior and senior years. It was during my senior year that my brother returned to Chicago from Vietnam. Jack had been in the 101st Airborne Division, a division which suffered almost half of all the American fatalities in Vietnam. He'd seen his share of action as a "grunt." I was delighted that he was returning unharmed. I went to the seminary rector to tell him that I needed to go to Chicago to welcome my brother home. He told me I couldn't go. I told him I wasn't asking. I was merely informing him that I'd be in Chicago when my brother's plane landed. Needless to say, the rector and I didn't reach a mutually acceptable understanding. I was voted out of the seminary after my senior year but the vote was over-turned by the provincial and his advisory council. So I went on to the Catholic Theological Union in Chicago for graduate studies. Four years later, in 1974, I was ordained a priest, culminating thirteen years of seminary travel/travail.

As so I was released into full-time ministry, although

67

"unleashed" might be more accurate. I was filled with the self-righteousness of the crusader. I would proclaim the "gospel" of contemporary theology to all. I would "vanquish" those outmoded theologies which people still clung to out in "the vineyard." Holding high the banner of radical religion, I would slay the beast of narrow-minded traditionalism. Bearing the armor of Karl Rahner and Hans Kung, I would valiantly withstand every volley of right-wing arrows. I was certain the world was waiting for me!

I was wrong. Zealots are not easily endured. One good thing, however, is that I got to move frequently during my early years in priesthood. I became a clerical rolling stone. It took some time to "exorcise" the "demon" who relished pushing people into the innovative, shocking them into the new. I imagined people would want to escape fear-based faith as much as I did. Having decided what path people should be on, I was determined to get them there regardless of protest. Actually, I was a pain in the ass.

We, who serve the church as priests, need to offer a variety of religious paths to our people. Problems happen when church officials, such as pastors, proclaim only this road or that road can be taken. Our people get understandably confused. Father So and So says this is what must be believed. Father Such and Such says this is what we must believe. We who serve in church leadership roles often promote our

Fashioning a Healthier Religion

personal theologies as revealed truth. We could all use a gentler hand.

Those of us who are pastors need to be careful not to abuse our parishioners by giving them a pre-packaged faith instead of offering pathways. What we do as parish priests and pastoral ministers is point out possible paths, while being aware of the path we are personally traveling. While we may prefer our own path, we need to respect everyone's right to choose a different one. We don't respect the people we serve unless we acknowledge their right to tred paths different from our own. Those of us who are "liberal" need to value those who are "conservative" and vice versa. We need to quit calling each other names, fighting over how best to come to God.

It's difficult being a priest today. If we're conservative, we're beset by liberals. If we're liberal, we're attacked by conservatives. If we're moderate, we're assailed from both right and left. It's no wonder, then, that many of us try to appease as many people as we can, having become weary of religious "wars." And we often attempt appeasement by being religiously innocuous. We lack the courage needed to speak the gospel simply and directly. As Urban T. Holmes mentions in *The Priest in Community:*

> What such a priest (weak-ineffectual) offers is like "junk cereal." It tastes sweet, it gives us something to crunch on, and our appetite is appeased for the moment, while

69

Thomas Aldworth

all the time we are dying from religious malnutrition. The lack of priestly nerve, cloaked behind a sugar coating, is demonic. It destroys people because it does not help them face the dark corners of their own lives.

I'm sure there have been times when I offered a "cotton candy" God to people. I suspect many of us priests pretend from time to time that the Hound of Heaven is really a dachshund.

My role as priest is to help people stand against whatever opponents their lives reveal. For many years now, I've been involved in the Korean martial art of Taekwondo, which is very similar to karate. I'm currently a third degree black belt in this discipline. I've fought in a good number of tournaments over the years. My nose has been broken as well as a few toes. I've had more bumps and bruises than I care to remember. Being Irish, I figure such pain is a way of atoning for the sins of my youth!

In Taekwondo fights, a chest protector is worn, as well as arm pads, shin pads and a head protector. This protection is meant to prevent most serious injuries. I see my role as priest-pastor to help people put on the protection they need to fight the enemies they face in life. I also encourage them, cheering them on as they stand against whatever they would rather hide or run from. Adversaries come in all shapes and sizes. Sometimes one fights doubts. Other times, various fears. Now and then, evil itself. Maybe an occasional

70

wrestling match with God, like Jacob and his angel. Perhaps Paul had this in mind when he wrote 1 Corinthians 9:26-27:

> That is why I am like a boxer, who does not waste his punches. I harden my body with blows and bring it under complete control, to keep myself from being disqualified after having called others to the contest. (*New Catholic Study Bible* translation)

The only way those of us who are priests can become true pastors is by being willing to risk standing in the open, away from all hiding places. When I was a child, my favorite hiding place was my mother's closet. Whenever something would frighten me, I would hide out in her closet, safe and secure behind her clothes. But hiding places are primarily for kids. If we have too many hiding places as adults, we miss the lushness of life. Being out in the open, being vulnerable, is risky but there's greater danger in being addicted to hiding places. The priest must be the one who shuns hiding places. As Holmes notes:

> For a priest to possess authority, he must be vulnerable to others. He must show his soul. The tragic irony is that the perversion of authority, against which so many rebel, comes out of the need to do just the opposite: to hide behind status within the institution.

For us to experience God, we have to become vulnerable to him. I'm becoming convinced as I progress through life that God is something of a celestial

71

boxer. We live our lives with so many defenses that God finds it difficult coming close to us. He must, in a sense, attack us. He seems especially fond of using beauty-filled fists. He pummels us until we relinguish our defenses and "surrender" to him.

In our "God-fight," however, we should offer a reasonable contest. In my years of Taekwondo, I've especially enjoyed those bouts where my competitor was equal to or better than myself. I was invigorated by a challenging match. I suspect God might be "invigorated" in a similar way. Maybe the life of faith involves becoming strong enough to let God hit us with his best punch.

I envision God as the undefeated opponent whom I must face from time to time. The more times I face him, the more determined I become to put up a good fight. I will lose but I wish to go down fighting. Like Rocky in his first movie, I just want to stay in the ring until the final bell. Maybe God just wants us to enter the ring with him despite our fears. Maybe faith grows each time we step into God's boxing ring.

Many of the fears that keep us from encountering God revolve around our understanding of sin. Sin would somehow keep God from loving us. Sin would "offend" God. Sin would eternally condemn us to hell-fire. There's still so much confusion about sin. As Albert Nolan mentions in *God in South Africa:*

Fashioning a Healthier Religion

Sin is not a very popular word today. It conjures up visions of punishment and hell and produces neurotic feelings of guilt and seems to be chiefly a matter of sex. I wonder if there is any other word in the Christian vocabulary which has been so thoroughly misused and whose meaning has been so completely distorted.

When I was taught about sin in grade school, it seemed sin was everywhere. We went to confession every Saturday because we assumed a person couldn't get though a week without significant sin. We got caught in understanding sin as being linked to certain emotions such as anger and sexual desire. If we got angry with our parents or our siblings, we had to confess it as a sin. But a serious injustice was done to us when we were told that God wouldn't like us if we got angry—that it was a sin.

Anger needs to be acknowledged as a strong emotion but it shouldn't be shamed as sinful. Anger is the normal emotional reaction to feeling hurt or having our boundaries violated. Not to feel anger would be hazardous. It's a necessary survival tool, divinely planted within us. Emotions such as anger and sexual desire are not the result of original sin but rather the handiwork of our Maker. To claim they're sinful is to imply the Creator mishandled creation.

To teach our children it's wrong or sinful to feel any emotion is a grave injustice. Feelings are morally neutral. They aren't usually under a great deal of conscious control and anything not under conscious control can't be deemed sinful. Sin is a self-conscious evil. We can't sin by accident.

Many parents teach their children they shouldn't feel a certain way. If their child is afraid, they may say "You shouldn't be afraid . . . big boys (girls) don't feel that way!" But such statements confuse children. The reality of the emotion is then denied. The Swiss psychoanalyst, Alice Miller, writes about the damage that can happen when a child's emotions get repressed. In *The Drama of the Gifted Child* she notes: "It is precisely because a child's feelings are so strong that they cannot be repressed without serious consequences." For a child to attempt suppressing feelings labeled "bad" or "sinful" is a destructive act against the self which Miller calls "soul murder." She talks about the personality generated when such attempts to suppress feelings are successful:

> They (people with narcissistic disturbances resulting from suppressing childhood feelings) are never overtaken by unexpected emotions and will only admit those feelings that are accepted by their inner censor, which is their parent's heir. Depression and a sense of inner emptiness is the price they must pay for this control.

I spent a few years hearing confessions at St. Peter's Church in downtown Chicago. In those years I heard

Fashioning a Healthier Religion

thousands of confessions. Many of the confessions bothered me because I'd hear the ways people had been religiously led into denying emotions. People often confessed getting angry. I'd try to explain that feeling angry wasn't sinful in itself. It's what we did with our anger that determined sin. Feeling angry by itself wasn't sinful but if we abused our spouse or children because of our angry feeling, then we would enter the realm of sin. Sometimes people got angry because of my explanation about anger.

Another emotion encountered frequently during my years as a full-time confessor was penitents' sexual feelings. People would often confess that they had "entertained impure thoughts." I still cannot hear "I entertained impure thoughts" without smiling. As I wondered in *Shaping a Healthy Religion,* "where does one take an impure thought to entertain it?"

Most of us were taught in Catholic grade school that we could wind up in hell because of impure thoughts. If we thought about the cute girl in the next row, we might be in dire straits. If we saw a "suggestive" show on television, we might find ourselves sliding into perdition. At least in the high school seminary my classmates and I would be protected from such dangerous mental "meanderings."

I think we damaged ourselves by proclaiming we couldn't or shouldn't have sexual thoughts. After all, without sexual thoughts, there would be a quick end to our species. Yet many of us struggled for years with sexual thoughts, trying to batter them into conscious control. Many the attitude conveyed by her have abandoned our church because of insistence that each sexual thought be accounted for in confession lest be burn eternally. Many of us have had an experience akin to that described by Richard Gilman in *Faith, Sex, Mystery:*

> When I began to confess "impure" thoughts I was more often than not asked questions like "How many times have you committed this sin?" (I remember on one occasion when after I'd replied "Four times, Father," I had to resist the temptation to amend that with "No, three and a half, I nipped one of them in the bud"), and "Are you married?" (this, of course, to ascertain if I was a first or second degree wretch), and "Do you take brisk walks or cold showers at such times?" (twice I was asked that), and when these were followed by admonitions to "rid" myself of my mental offenses against God, my irritation, doubt and uncertainty grew.

We're still reaping the spoiled fruits of a long history of attacks on sexual desire. Some of these attacks arose from Greek philosophy, as Brundage relates:

> The truly wise person, according to Stoic teachings, cultivated a sober and reserved demeanor; he ab-

stained from sex and other lower concerns, such as eating and drinking, beyond the minimum essential for bodily health. Accordingly, the wise man should strive to control his reactions to sensual stimuli, including erotic sensations. He should not, for example, be aroused by the sight of his neighbor's wife in the nude; rather he should censor these base feelings and discipline his reactions to bodily sensations. This mastery of the mind should be maintained even in marriage; *it is wrong to lust after another man's wife, but it is equally wrong to lust after one's own.*

So what may seem to be early Christian teaching on sin may actually be Greek Stoic philosophy. "The Stoics generally disapproving view of sex rested on their belief that human reason vanished during the sex act." But it wasn't only the Stoics who disapproved of sexual desire. As Brundage continues:

> Sex, he (Plato) maintained in the *Republic,* trapped men in a bog of sensuality, from which they found it difficult, or even impossible, to escape. Hence wise men should shun sex altogether or at least be wary of its allures.

Even Aristotle, according to Brundage, believed "the desirable kind of love, the truly human kind, was love that transcended physical desire and sexual passion, love that was cool, rational, and nonsexual."

It's no surprise then that the early church wound up with the sexual teachings of Jerome and Augustine. These saints based their moral proscriptions on the teachings of Plato, Aristotle and the Stoics. As Brundage notes:

> St. Jerome maintained that sex and salvation were contradictions. Even in marriage, coitus was evil and unclean, Jerome thought, and married Christians should avoid sexual contact whenever possible.

He continues:

> Sexual desire, Augustine believed, was the most foul and unclean of human wickednesses, the most pervasive manifestation of man's disobedience to God's designs.

There's no doubt that Jerome and Augustine were among the most influential theologians in the first thousand years of our church. Augustine may have had more influence on the development of our Christian theology than anyone else. Much of what he wrote is wonderful. His appreciation of God's loving presence is magnificent. His recognition of the hunger we have for God is one of the most profound insights we've been given. But his views on sexuality have damaged all of us who came after him. It's too easy to explain away his sexual beliefs as the result of his own life-story. Much of what he taught arose from the prevailing philosophies of his time and not only from personal struggles with sex and the devastating death of his son, Adeodatus, which he believed was a punishment from God for his sexual behavior.

It wasn't only our feelings that came under attack in grade school. We also had to be on guard against the thoughts that wafted through our heads. We were taught it was as sinful to think something evil as to actually do it. If we thought about robbing a bank, we were as guilty as if we'd actually carried out the robbery. If we fantasized about having intercourse with someone, we were as culpable as any actual fornicator. Yet fantasies may serve an important purpose in the machinations of the mind. They may foster creativity and even serve as a "pressure valve" for antisocial and violent tendencies.

I'd certainly rather have someone think about killing me than to actually do it. I can't see how these two "sins" are equal. Thoughts often just "bubble up" within our psyches. Some of the thoughts may be wild and irresponsible. Some of them may be evil and dangerous. But the thoughts themselves are not as sinful as actually following through on the thoughts.

We'll certainly have "lustful" thoughts regularly. Because of our genetic structure, we'll be excited by other people. I can't imagine getting too worried about this normal human reaction. Remember the furor created when President Carter admitted in a *Playboy* interview that he had "lustful thoughts."

79

Thomas Aldworth

Would we really want a president who didn't have lustful thoughts, a president beyond the bounds of normalcy?

Our feelings and thoughts are vital to our sense of self, our self-esteem. If our feeling and thoughts are belittled, then we lose our self identity. We become alienated from who we really are. Yet it's precisely here that our church in particular and religion in general helped distort who we are. We were taught to be afraid of our own feelings, our own thoughts. They were potentially sinful, offensive to God. Only "good" thoughts and feelings were allowed. "Bad" thoughts and feelings had to be suppressed and confessed. Consequently, many of us become afraid of ourselves. Not only were "bad" thoughts sinful, they could drag us into hell. We'd have to be always vigilant. But because we became vigilantes against our very selves, wholeness and happiness became impossible. The part of ourself deemed "bad" was banished. But, as Alice Miller maintains: "It is not only the 'beautiful,' 'good' and pleasant feelings that make us really alive, deepen our existence and give us crucial insight but precisely the unacceptable and unadapted ones from which we would prefer to escape."

Now I'm not suggesting we should be raised socially irresponsible. All of us need to be taught a sense of right and wrong, to develop our consciences. Our children's consciences need to be cultivated as they grow. We surely have enough people already with no sense of moral guilt, no idea of right or wrong, without adding more. But teaching our children about sin and social responsibility without damaging their self-esteem is decidedly difficult. We need to be careful not to imply to them that there's a part of their personality they must get rid of if God is to love them fully.

Those of us professionally involved with religion need to be more tolerant of the "dark side" of our own human psyche. Perhaps we should settle for an uneasy truce rather than seek unconditional victory over whatever part of our personality is deemed "bad" or sinful. Perhaps we should accept our imperfection and not expect perfection this side of heaven. Demanding perfection of ourselves and our children leads to a life of unredemptive suffering. As Alan Jones reminds us in *Soul Making:*

> The true believer is often bedeviled by a neurotic aim at perfection. Indeed, it is accepted in psychoanalytical circles that perfectionism inhibits human growth and saps our capacity for delighting in life. And yet the great demand of religion is, of course, "Be ye perfect."

Sin is a human reality. We must continue to struggle with the very real oppressiveness of sin. We need to proclaim loudly the social consequences of our sinful action and sinful inaction. We probably need, however, to break the connection between sin and subsequent divine punishment. To teach that God will punish us because of our sin has crippled us and prevented us from traveling very far on our journey to God.

A few years ago, I was standing atop the marvelous Cliffs of Moher on the west coast of Ireland. The cliffs rise hundreds of feet out of the Atlantic. It's a spectacular vantage-point for sunsets. That particular evening, I was the only person on the cliffs. I saw a small boat being rowed by a single man, heading towards the Aran Islands some 20 miles away. I watched the man for a long time. He and his boat appeared so small in the ocean's vastness. From where I watched, he didn't seem to be making much progress towards the islands. Yet he kept rowing. As darkness descended, I lost sight of him. By then, however, he was far out in the ocean and much closer to his destination. Perhaps we are spiritual kin to that lone rower. Much of our past training, especially concerning sin, has kept us from putting both oars in the water. We wound up either going in circles or else being at the mercy of the waves. A healthier understanding of sin will enable us to use both oars as we row our boat on the great ocean of God.

CHAPTER FOUR

Priests and Sacramental Ministry

THE DAY I was brought new-born home from the hospital, my Aunt Mamie declared I had the hands of a priest. I was told this tale many times as I grew. I'm not sure if it was meant to encourage me to consider priesthood but I didn't need any encouragement. I wanted to be a priest from a very early age, deciding it was my best chance for getting to heaven. Our parish priests were also neighborhood heroes. Most of us boys in the urban Catholic neighborhoods of the past dreamed at least occasionally of becoming a priest. Such dreams were more frequent for those of us who were altar boys. We all wanted to be like Bing Crosby in *Going My Way* and *The Bells of St. Mary's*, "crooning" our way into the heart of God.

My mother, growing up in Ireland, was given a stern view of priests. She'd have to step into the street if there was a priest walking toward her on the sidewalk. She wasn't supposed to share the sidewalk with him. I wasn't raised with such a subservient view of priests but I did respect them. They seemed to belong

Thomas Aldworth

to some sort of secret but sacred society. I wanted to be one of them. But our grade school Sisters told us God would have to call us if we were going to be priests. We had to have a "vocation."

I've pretty much abandoned the idea of God calling people to priesthood or other professions. God has hopes and dreams for all his children but they're multi-dimensional. There are many ways to "live out" his hopes and dreams. I believe people are attracted to priesthood the same way people are attracted to the professions of fire-fighting or teaching. The notion of God having a set plan for each person strikes me as too narrow and deterministic. Perhaps God's dream for us is the one from Micah 6:8: "This is what God asks of you, only this: to act justly, to love tenderly and to walk humbly with your God." (Jerusalem Bible translation) Such is our true vocation. Such is the dream God has for each of his children.

If I'd left the seminary (or been asked to leave) before completing my thirteen years of study, I don't believe God would have been "disappointed." His dream for me is not limited by the profession I choose. It'd be egotistic for me to believe that God somehow hand-picked me for priesthood, that he "plucked" me out of the crowd. While such a belief would be profoundly affirming, it would also be psychologically damaging. I'd begin considering myself as divinely appointed.

Fashioning a Healthier Religion

All of us want to feel "chosen." We all want to feel we're special in God's eyes. We want to believe God pointed his finger at us and said "I Want You!" like a heavenly Uncle Sam. The fact is we're all equally "special" in God's eyes. He doesn't have favorites.

The idea of being "chosen" has induced some of us priests to abuse the power that comes with our office. If God has "picked" us, then he must also have endowed us with extraordinary wisdom and unquestionable authority. We can "lord" it over others, since we are "other Christs." The potential for abuse is high, especially when it comes to the dispensing of sacraments. In the movie "The Rosary Murders," for exampl, the pastor refuses to baptize a baby because the mother is unmarried. The "hero" of the movie, Father Koestler, goes ahead and baptizes the baby regardless.

While there's a legitimate need to ascertain if a child will be raised Catholic prior to baptizing, we need to be reticent denying the sacrament to anyone. Often a new-born will bring parents back to regular church worship. To deny parents permission to baptize their baby because they are irregular church-goers (or contributors) can precipitate a complete break with the church. We priests shouldn't "scold" those who wish to return to full church participation—yet that's exactly what's done in many instances. We get all excited and start claiming the only reason they're coming

85

back is to have their baby baptized. So what? Maybe that's how God's grace works—giving parents a chance to examine their lives with the birth of a daughter or son. If their baby brings them back to church, shouldn't we be happy rather than play the harpy? Shouldn't we celebrate instead of wagging our finger in their faces?

We priests should also be cautious in deciding who can and can't be married. While we're expected to make an evaluation based on interviews and marriage assessment instruments, we should be extremely hesitant telling two people they aren't "meant for each other." There are, of course, legitimate reasons why some couples shouldn't marry. Perhaps a pregnancy has brought two people to the altar when they wouldn't have been there otherwise. I remember one of the first weddings I performed. A woman and her mother came to me about arranging a wedding. The potential bride was pregnant. I set up a meeting for the couple and their parents. When we were all together, I mentioned that even though a pregnancy was involved, we should make sure these two people really wanted to marry. Well, the woman's father looked stricken. No one had told him his daughter was "with child." We muddled through the rest of the meeting but I wasn't pleased with being the one to convey such information. But the wedding went on.

I've married couples who I thought would be strong

in their marriage who didn't survive two years together. There have been other couples who I felt had little hope of happy marriages who have surprised me with the depth of their commitment. Deciding those couples with "good" marriage potential and those with "bad" marriage potential is a delicate business, worthy of Solomon. We priests should recognize our limitations even if we presume Solomon's wisdom.

Naturally, those of us who pastor churches need to make sure we have worthwhile pre-marriage programs. These programs are usually conducted by married couples from the parish, often those who have participated in some form of "Marriage Encounter." These pre-marriage, or pre-cana, programs can be very beneficial to couples seeking marriage. But beyond arranging effective pre-marriage programs, priests should be incredibly cautious in making pre-marital judgments. I'm not convinced we have the right to decide who can or can't marry. Except in cases of psychological pathology or obvious immaturity, who marries who is, frankly, none of our business.

The reason why we continue to assume it's our business, though, is because we see marriage as a once only affair. If a marriage doesn't work out, there are no other marriages permitted for life. A divorced twenty-five year old mother with two small children must remain alone, even though she may meet a man who could create a loving family environment for her and her children. A divorced middle-aged man withering away in loneliness will just have to wither away. Or else we create people who "flit" from affair to affair, masking their unwillingness to permanently commit with the complaint that they're prevented from remarriage by the church. An elderly woman, unable to get along on her fixed income, can't remarry since she never received an annulment. How many people are waiting for the death of their ex-spouse so they can be free to marry in the church? The number of such people and their pain surely screams to heaven. What kind of church have we created when it's easier to receive absolution for having your ex-spouse killed than it is to receive an annulment?

Our church declares you cannot remarry unless your first marriage is deemed invalid. Even if you've never been married, you can't marry someone who has been validly married before. Even if a Catholic wants to marry a divorced Protestant, the Protestant person will need an annulment before marriage in the church is possible. For someone to receive an annulment, usually a rather lengthy process must be undergone. There exists a wide-spread, although erroneous, belief that annulments can be "arranged" if a person is important or wealthy. Even though this is a false notion, a good many people have the illusion that annulments can be "bought."

Fashioning a Healthier Religion

An annulment is granted when it's proven that a marriage as understood by the church never happened. Basically there are three intentions required for a marriage to be valid in the Catholic Church. Couples getting married are familiar with these intentions since they must sign a statement declaring: 1) they intend this marriage to be life-long, 2) they intend to be faithful to each other, and 3) they are open to the possibility of children (naturally dependent upon age—not required of elderly couples). If these three intentions are not present, there can be no valid marriage regardless what happens in church or on the honeymoon. If either person is forced into the marriage for any reason or if either can't competently understand what's intended by the three intentions due to immaturity or psychological make-up, the marriage can also be annulled.

Procuring an annulment is a complicated and time-consuming project. There are many people working in the tribunals of every diocese, trying to handle the enormous number of annulment requests. Some tribunals are progressive. Some are not. Being granted an annulment depends a bit on where a person lives. It also depends on finding a parish priest willing to put in the time and energy required to prepare the annulment case prior to its being presented to the tribunal.

I've heard of people who make an annulment more

possible through pre-marriage maneuvering. They openly announce they'll seek a divorce if the marriage doesn't work out or they'll sign a statement to that effect. The witnesses or the statement can then be produced when and if an annulment becomes necessary. In other words, they "hedge" their marriage bet. They also enter a canonically invalid marriage.

A church annulment only has ecclesiastical effects. While an annulment declares that in the eyes of the church a marriage never existed, civil law must also be considered. The annulment process cannot begin without a civil divorce decree. A declaration of nullity also does nothing to the legitimate/legal status of children born during the marriage.

Many people in our church have the mistaken assumption that divorced people are barred from participating in Eucharist. They believe an excommunication accompanies divorce. Such is not the case. Ecclesiastical penalties come only with remarriage outside the church when a couple can't or won't get an annulment prior to remarriage. Without church permission for the remarriage, it will be judged an invalid marriage and the couple will usually be perceived as "living in sin." They'll often be denied the right to receive communion. If they go to confession, they may be told they can receive communion only if they're willing to live together as brother and sister with no sexual contact. It's no surprise when people in such circumstances grudgingly leave the church.

Most parish priests do what they can. They usually try first for an official annulment decree. If that proves impossible, perhaps because of unavailable witnesses, priests will often try to resolve the remarriage within the context of conscience. Since conscience is paramount, if people honestly believe their first marriage to be invalid and their present marriage to be valid in the eyes of God, then they're free to receive communion. As John Huels notes in *The Pastoral Companion:* "Any prudent doubt about either the gravity or the public nature of the sin should be resolved in favor of the person who wishes to receive Communion." And Barry Brunsman adds in *New Hope for Divorced Catholics:* "A sincere Catholic remarried 'outside the Church' can never be prohibited from receiving Communion."

Sometime soon we'll finally have to see the notion of indissoluble marriage as an exemplary ideal, while accept that some marriages just end. Often I've experienced couples coming into my office, dragging the dead body of their marriage behind them. They expect me to resurrect the corpse even though too many fatal blows have been inflicted. They presume because of the church's stand on indissolubility that I'll suggest hanging on to the remains of their marriage even when it's begun to decompose. Sometimes they just want me to be the one who declares the death of their marriage.

In other instances, however, couples bring in their marriage with life still clinging to it. Then we can attempt rehabilitation, especially if both spouses are willing to care for the sick soul of their marriage. But if both parties aren't willing to do the work of marital recovery, then not much can be done. I fear many parish priests seek to "save" what's beyond salvage.

People need each other. We normally find our way to God through the gift and grace of others. Mistakes are made in marriages. They unravel for many reasons. It's best to leave such marital "unravelings" in the compassionate hands of God and allow people to enter second marriages when their first marriage dies. Counseling should be provided to help people learn what they can from a failed marriage but to condemn them to solitary lives because of the church's belief in indissolubility seems unwise and unjust.

Marriage is one of our church's seven sacraments. Its inclusion as one of the sacraments, however, involves a complicated history. As Brundage notes in *Law, Sex, and Christian Society in Medieval Europe:*

> Neither the New Testament nor the Patristic writers gave any indication that they counted marriage as a sacrament, as they did baptism and the Eucharist.

Fashioning a Healthier Religion

Although Augustine sometimes referred to marriage as a "sacramentum," his meaning in these passages was clearly much different from his application of the term to the eucharistic and baptismal rites. The belief that marriage was a sacrament appeared only much later.

We who are professional church people need to do whatever we can to help people live lives of love. Most people live out that life of love in marriage. It's true there are people who shouldn't marry, just as it's true that there are people too damaged to be loving parents. We're all wounded. The only difference between us is the extent of our wounds. Without the balm of loving relationships, we're doomed to a life of alienation and stifled growth. Marriage is, by and large, the place where we receive healing from our woundedness. Those of us who are priests, or "wounded healers" in the language of Henri Nouwen, should be acutely aware of both the need and the power of healing. If we priests continue to insist on the indissolubility of marriage, we may rightly lose our "wounded healer" status and become merely "wounded wounders."

There are so many good men and women condemned to a life of relative despair because of our church's marriage laws. I hope priests can assist them in their attempts to fashion loving lives when a first

Thomas Aldworth

attempt fails rather than condemning such attempts. As Joseph Girzone relates through his Jesus character in *Joshua:*

> Religion is beautiful only when it is free and flows from the heart. That is why you should guide and inspire but not legislate behavior. And to threaten God's displeasure when people do not follow your rules is being a moral bully and does no service to God.

Much of our church's reaction to divorce and remarriage stems from Jesus' statements concerning divorce found in Matthew 5:31-32; 19:3-13; Mark 10:2-13 and Luke 16:18. Jesus is portrayed in the Gospels as being opposed to a liberal interpretation of Mosaic law on divorce. Deuteronomy 24:3 allows divorce because of indecency or immorality. There was a great deal of debate at the time of Jesus, however, concerning what constituted acceptable grounds for divorce. There were two main schools of thought among the rabbis. As Brundage indicates:

> The School of Shammai adopted a restrictive position and taught that a man might divorce his wife only if she were guilty of unchastity, while the School of Hillel took a more permissive view and allowed divorce on many grounds, so that a husband who was dissatisfied with his wife's cooking, for example, could lawfully divorce her for that reason alone. Rabbi Akiba went so far as to declare that a man who sighted a woman more

beautiful than his wife was justified in repudiating his spouse and marrying the more attractive rival.

At the time of Jesus, only husbands could divorce their wives. Wives were prohibited from divorcing in Jewish law. There was an obvious inequity at work. I believe Jesus' pronouncements against divorce were meant to protect women from the injustice of losing their home because of a burnt supper or the appearance of an attractive woman. An enormous burden was placed upon a wife when her husband could divorce her so capriciously. I believe Jesus in his infinite compassion wanted to lift that burden from women's backs.

Still today women often suffer the greater brunt of the divorce process. They normally wind up less financially stable after the divorce. Often a wife is left with the children while the husband goes off looking for lost youth in the arms of a younger woman. I know too many women who have been left alone to care for their young. The prospect of a second marriage for these women is bleak at best. There aren't enough men willing to take on a couple of children as part of a marriage. But if the possibility of remarriage occurred for these women, I, for one, would congratulate them and strive in every way to make that marriage possible within the confines of the church.

Obviously, we shouldn't make it easier to renounce

Thomas Aldworth

marriage vows. Priests should aid couples in repairing what is repairable. I just think we should stop beating the proverbial "dead horse." What good can possibly come from staying in a marriage which produces only bitterness and pain? There's surely enough bitterness and pain in our world without condoning more. People often come to priests when they're suffering the most pain. Our priestly task is to diminish the suffering, not increase it through proclaiming laws and decrees. I recall reading a definition of "hero" as someone who suffers without passing it on to others; someone who absorbs suffering and declares that suffering stops with him or her. We priests shouldn't pass up this opportunity to be genuine heroes.

Our people's pain has sometimes been increased in the sacrament of reconciliation, or "confession"—as we used to call it. I'm not talking about the painful fear many of us have when we approach the confessional. I'm talking about the pain created by confessors who are filled with so much personal pain that it splashes on those who come to them for forgiveness. Too many of us have been yelled at in our confessionals. Too many of us have been verbally abused.

Kneeling down in the confessional or sitting face-to-face with the confessor, many of us regress to feeling like children. We sense the priest is there not only to forgive but also to judge. We've come to have our hands ritually slapped. There's often a rush of relief leaving the confessional or reconciliation room.

We continue to go to confession, though, because we believe unconfessed sin will keep us eternally from God. If we die with an unconfessed mortal sin, we'll supposedly spend eternity being battered and tormented by Satan and his hellish cohorts. We don't realize that the notion of "hell" was a rather late theological development. For most of the time before Jesus, Hebrew people believed that when a person died there was no further consciousness. A deceased person went to a place called "Sheol" but he or she didn't know they were there. There was no after-life awareness.

The prevailing theology of the time, therefore, contended the only way God could show his favor was in this life. If a person didn't sin and was faithful to the Torah, God would reward him or her with many possessions, long life and many children. If a person was poor, died young or was childless, he or she was being punished for their sins or the sins of their ancestors. And God apparently had a long memory regarding sin. Deuteronomy 23:3 states: "No one born out of wedlock or any descendant of such a person, *even in the tenth generation*, may be included among the Lord's people." Ten generations can produce a tremendous number of off-spring. Most of them probably, wouldn't even know they were barred from God's people.

Gradually over time, a theology of afterlife developed. God would be able to show his favor somewhere other than earthly life. Many Jewish people in the time of Jesus held to a place of reward in the next life as well as a place of punishment. Those who were faithful would spend eternity "in the bosom of Abraham." Those who were evil would spend eternity in a place called "Gehenna," which was Jerusalem's garbage dump where trash burned day and night.

Most Christians today no longer believe God will reward our sinlessness with possessions, long life and children. Jerry Falwell is an exception when he claims "Wealth is God's way of rewarding those who put him first." Most of us believe God will repay us for a life of relative sinlessness with a pass through the "pearly gates." However, he'll punish our sinfulness by routing us to hell's fire. As I mentioned in *Shaping a Healthy Religion*, I'm not a fan of eternal punishment places. I'm not convinced they have a legitimate place in Christian theology. While I believe in the possibility of choosing not to be with God forever, I don't believe such a place is akin to a medieval torture-chamber.

We deal with sin not because some Sword of

Fashioning a Healthier Religion

Damocles is perched over our heads but because sin prevents us from knowing the love intended for us. We no longer view sin the same way people did at the time of Jesus. They saw sin as a debt owing to God, who demanded some retribution, some "pound of flesh." Sickness was often seen as God's punishment for sins. But Jesus changed the prevalent belief in sin as a debt. Albert Nolan points out in *Jesus Before Christianity* that, in dealing with people: "Jesus overlooked their past and refused to hold anything at all against them. He treated them as people who were no longer, if ever, indebted to God and, therefore, no longer deserving of rejection and punishment."

We, who are confessors would do well to follow the example of Jesus in dealing compassionately with people. This need for compassion is especially vital with children. Children can easily develop images of God which will haunt them for life. We need to help them understand what sin is and why they should deal with it. We shouldn't unnerve them with tales of never-ending agony. There's plenty to be afraid of as a child without adding eternal infernos.

It's difficult being a good confessor. I don't yet possess the wisdom required. Basically, I just keep it simple. If the person wants to talk, fine, but otherwise I don't play the interrogator. I don't ask many

99

questions. I also try not to take what is confessed too personally. There are confessors who are upset by the sins they hear confessed. While I feel pain when I hear of violence and abuse, I don't get upset, for instance, when sexual sins are confessed. I don't feel any need to take a sexual history.

Are there sexual sins that might keep us eternally from God? There might be. I'm just not sure what they are. I'm sure that kissing more than ten seconds isn't a mortal sin, regardless what we were taught on Chicago's Southside. Sexuality and self-esteem are interwoven. Sexual "perversions" emanate more from childhood damage than from the temptations of roving devils. Understanding why people "act out" sexually would be more beneficial than being concerned with whether a sin is "venial" or "mortal."

An abundance of questions about a person's sexual life in confession may be an abuse of the sacrament. As I've already mentioned, I don't have much to say in confession. It's not that I'm unconcerned but I prefer appearing detached rather than probing where I don't belong. Penitents shouldn't be forced to answer questions that are too personal. Confessors don't have the right to demand intimate information.

Most of us confessors, of course, don't ask too many questions or make too many demands for disclosure. But we often appear disheartened by what the person may confess. We breathe a great sigh and admonish the person to do better in the future. We imply the person confessing is a wretch and we must now bear the weight of his or her sins. We seem to take it all too personally. It's like my twin brother driving his car. He's an aggressive driver. He considers it a personal affront if another car passes him on the expressway. Driving with him always helps me review my life, as I consider amending my wayward ways. Buckling myself into his car, "O, my God, I am heartily sorry" often springs to mind.

Those of us who are confessors sometimes give the impression that since we're celibate, we carry the burden of everyone's sexual sins. Confessors who are aware of their own weakness usually aren't surprised or oppressed by the weakness of others. Those who find it difficult acknowledging personal weakness are usually the harshest confessors. But they're also harsh with themselves. They often end up isolated from their very selves since they're unable to accept their own brokenness, their "shadow." Confessors deal with other's deficiencies in the same way they deal with their own. Or as James Baldwin said it: "One can only accept in others what one can accept in oneself."

Gentleness is the hallmark of a good confessor.

Thomas Aldworth

I don't have that gentleness yet. I can be a grouchy confessor. Often my grouchiness comes from hearing people unable to confront sin in a healthy manner because of either arrogance or misplaced guilt. I also get grouchy when people come to confession vexed with some variety of spiritual masochism. These are the people who want the confessor to be upset with them. They want to be yelled at. I also feel grumpy when men and women confess "playing with themselves." I remember not knowing whether to laugh or cry when I heard a man confess that he "played with" himself two and a half times. I debated asking what "the half" meant but I decided silence was the more charitable response.

I'm happy there aren't many adolescents any longer confessing either sexual thoughts or masturbation. I don't know whether our young are finally understanding sexual thoughts as a normal part of the human psyche or if they're refusing to deal with sexual sin at all. Masturbation, which continues to be one of the sins most confessed in males over forty, doesn't seem to be considered confessional material in younger males. I hope our young are developing healthier ideas of what is seriously sinful and what is not.

I'm not saying that sexual expression in our young isn't an important ethical issue. It certainly is. Much of what is demanded in the name of love isn't bad.

Fashioning a Healthier Religion

Self-esteem is so fragile in adolescence that many are manipulated into going where they'd rather not go. Innocence isn't bad. The instant intimacy which appears as a quick fix to our pain and problems isn't very healing. But, by and large, our institutions haven't been very helpful in assisting our young develop sane sexual norms.

To help our young fashion a balanced sexual ethics will be a prodigious task. I'm not sure how to accomplish it but I know that shaming our young is not part of a sane sexuality or a sensible spirituality. We'll probably have to re-examine much of our Christian tradition. We still have some strange sexual ethics roaming about, perhaps reflecting people like St. John Cassian. As Brundage notes:

> St. John Cassian considered masturbation and nocturnal pollution central issues in sexual morality . . . he believed that the frequency of erotic dreams and nocturnal erections and emissions were indices of lust. A monk or hermit, he reasoned, might be able to overcome overt sexual temptations, but if he continued to experience sexual fantasies in dreams, and if he continued to have seminal emissions during sleep, then he had not yet overcome carnal lust. Hence, both his religious life and his salvation might be in peril.

I'm glad I wasn't a monk during those days. Yet many of us were taught to fear our own thoughts if we were to hope for heaven. We allowed the vital force of eros to be way-laid on the road to salvation.

As I remarked in *Shaping a Healthy Religion*, masturbation was seen in the not-too-distant past as a mortal sin because of a faulty understanding of physiology. Until about a hundred years ago, sperm was believed to contain the complete child. Mothers were mere "incubators" for the sperm. Masturbation was thus regarded as akin to abortion, the destruction of a complete child. Masturbation, accordingly, became a mortal sin "heavyweight." As Karl Menninger noted in *Whatever Became of Sin?*: "To an extent difficult for the present-day reader to grasp, this was the major sin for middle- and upper-class adolescents a century and less ago."

Masturbation can, of course, become excessive, pointing to a possible narcissistic wound or even true pathology. Masturbation can also short-circuit the indispensable human quest for intimacy. But, normally, masturbation isn't something to get very excited about in confession. A married man might masturbate because of his wife's absence or unavailability. There's no reason to make such a penitent feel as if he's reverting to adolescent behavior. Some married people, of course, may masturbate as an act of hostility against their spouse, deciding not to pursue marital intimacy. Or they may masturbate rather than risk repetitious rejections by their spouse. Such cases require judicious counsel rather than sermonettes about the supposed evils of masturbation.

I'm not suggesting doing whatever we fell like doing. Acting out our fantasies would lead to disastrous results. Impulsiveness often has tragic consequences. But we should be careful with our passions. We cannot assassinate our sexual feelings without killing off all other feelings. Becoming a zombie certainly isn't the pathway to wholeness or holiness. We can't become people of compassion without retaining personal passion.

After people confess their sins, they are usually given a penance by the priest. The penance is meant to show the penitent's desire for conversion, as well as trying to "right the wrong." The penance is meant to balance the evil generated by the sin. Most penances, however, involve prayers. A person may be told to say "ten Our Fathers and ten Hail Mary's" as a penance or even to say a rosary if they've been especially "bad." A friend of mine told me she was given the entire New Testament to read as a penance. I didn't ask what she had confessed.

Penances can even be cruel. I know of a woman who confessed having had an abortion. Her confessor demanded she go look at the new-born babies in the maternity ward of the local hospital. While abortion is an obvious evil, that evil isn't balanced by mixing it with cruelty.

Thomas Aldworth

I've also heard of unusual penances. Another friend of mine was told to take a bubble bath as a penance. Perhaps the penance was given as a way of building self-esteem. Maybe the confessor imagined himself a "liberal" confessor. I'd have to quell a chuckle if a priest told me to take a bubble bath for my penance.

Giving penances is a difficult process. I'm not happy giving prayers as a penance because the person might get the idea that praying is a penance. I often ask people to spend a few minutes thanking God for their forgiveness, emphasizing that God is the one doing the forgiving, not the confessor. I'm still not content, though, with "giving thanks" as a penance. I've sometimes asked people what they'd like to do as a penance but often such a question only startles people and makes them feel uncomfortable.

With children, I usually have them do something special for someone in their family. They can help their mother or father with something they normally wouldn't help with. Or else I might tell them to do their best to avoid fights with their brothers or sisters for the next day or two. Having grown up with two brothers, I know avoiding sibling fights can be a taxing penance. I avoid telling children to say prayers as their penance, wanting to avoid linking prayer and penance.

Fashioning a Healthier Religion

Anyway, I'm still working on penances. Maybe when I get older and wiser, I'll come across some sound penance strategies. Actually, I'd be happier if I could just help people acquire a healthier view of sin; one that enabled them to raise their eyes to God rather than continually bowing their heads and beating their breasts. God doesn't point his finger at us like an accusing parent. He doesn't record all our sins like some cosmic accountant.

Becoming a helpful confessor is one of the more demanding tasks of priests, requiring tons of patience and compassion. We, confessors, either embrace penitents with God's unwavering, unconditional love or else we infect them with our own insecurities. We either hug them with the Father's forgiveness or mug them with our own fears.

If Bonaventure was right about sacraments being medicine for the soul, then those of us who ritualize the sacraments are spiritual physicians. Our duty involves healing as much as any doctor. We enable our parishioners to recover from the wounds of society through the healing energy of our parish communities. With the grace-filled oils of sacramental life, we massage the tired and torn muscles of our people. Through pastoral encouragement, we embolden them to stand against the enemies of life and love. Through our own experience of the Almighty, we revive an appreciation for the mystical.

Thomas Aldworth

In some respects, I'm not sure my Aunt Mamie's prediction wasn't a curse rather than a blessing. I've struggled for almost two decades with the "cloak" of priesthood. I suspect my struggle will last my life but perhaps the danger of priesthood lies in becoming too comfortable with it. Maybe priesthood is meant to "plague" the person who embraces it.

CHAPTER FIVE

Through Priestly Eyes

ABOUT ten years ago, I decided to spend my vacation traveling Greyhound buses from Cleveland to the Pacific Northwest. I'd been riding for almost two days when I arrived in Salt Lake City. Deciding on a few hours layover, I went looking for a shower. The roughly four billion organisms that normally live on and within us (we're never really alone) had probably doubled during my days on the bus.

I walked over to the Catholic cathedral rectory, figuring it was the best place to seek a shower. Knocking on the door, a religious Sister answered. I told her I was a priest and that I would like to take a shower if I could. She blanched and stammered for me to wait. A moment later a priest came and asked me what I wanted. I told him I was a Franciscan priest who'd been riding the Greyhound for two days and needed a shower. "Oh, a Franciscan," he smiled. I guess Franciscan priests are more inclined than diocesan priests to show up derelict-like at cathedral rectories. Anyway, I got my shower!

Belonging to a religious order, I'm a member of a

109

fraternity, a community. The loneliness inherent in celibacy is supposed to be eased by having brothers. I've found this to be true even though fraternity doesn't automatically happen just because religious men live together. The biggest blessing of community living, however, is the possibility of dealing intimately with each other.

We who are priests and brothers often hide from intimacy. But the intimate demands of responsible love are difficult for all people. Why should religious not find the demands of intimacy as arduous as anyone else? As Rainer Marie Rilke told us: "For one human being to love another, that is perhaps the most difficult of all our tasks, the ultimate, that last test and proof, the work for which all other work is but preparation."

All religious men and women are called to be loving people. But loving is a perilous journey. I know I'm not very good at it. Loving frightens me. Anyone who isn't a bit frightened by love probably hasn't come too close to it. Loving is hard work. It's easier to get wrapped up in some other, less exacting labor. Or we can always succumb to workaholism, one of the best defenses against love.

We priests need to love as best we can while acknowledging that we probably do it poorly. Priests are commissioned to be lovers, though not in the sexual sense. Celibacy is meant to enable us to embrace

110

Fashioning a Healthier Religion

love more easily instead of ignoring love's summons. We priests and religious would well heed the warning from Jones in *Soul Making:* "There are those who think they love God because they don't love anyone else. This seems to be an occupational hazard for religious people."

Priests and religious are "outsiders" to a degree. We're removed from the process of coupling which fuels much socializing. We're meant to love without conditions, without any desire to possess the person loved. When we're able to love unconditionally, we reveal God's nature to our people.

Having gone through college during the days of "flower power," I know it's easy to talk about love. All of us want to be loving, yet many of us refuse to undertake the psychic search needed to expose the ways we inflate our egos with false claims of loving. As Jones cautions: "Loving is hard and perilous, and there are many counterfeits. Part of soulmaking involves the willingness to sort out the true from the false and to face those inner cravings for control, security, and affection that masquerade as love."

We vowed celibates should be careful not to imply that celibacy is about sex. It's about opening our hearts to others. If being celibate doesn't make us more loving, what value does it have? If celibacy only makes us grumpy, what grace is there in that? Celibacy involves transforming the loneliness which is part and

Thomas Aldworth

parcel of our human condition. Loneliness is an emotion genetically programmed into us which pushes us into involvement with others. If we stay uninvolved, we suffer the pangs of loneliness. Loneliness pounds on our door until we finally open it.

The loneliness of celibates can be as devastating as the loneliness of late-night lounges. Unless we celibates locate companions to accompany us on our journey, the pain will be too much to bear. We'll have to ease the suffering one way or another, often in some addictive process. While priests and religious normally have contact with many people, we'll still suffer the torment of loneliness unless we find intimate friends with whom we can share our struggles and sorrows. We need supportive companions who will also be challenging. We need faithful friends who will assure us from time to time that we can be asinine. Such assurances are precious.

Celibates need to remember that we're celibate in order to have a space for God, an emptiness for him. If we don't allow God to fill that space, we'll be forced to fill it with anything or anyone handy. Nature abhors vacuums. We may try to fill the space with power and prestige or with busyness and work. We may try filling the space with numerous affairs.

When the empty space is filled with God, however, we're becoming the loving people we're meant to be. Being filled by God doesn't mean we excusing ourselves from loving others. The more we're filled with God's loving presence, the more loving we become to all. And to become loving is our most sacred task. If we fail at love, all our successes will be empty. As the 19th century Danish theologian Soren Kierkegaard warned us: "To cheat oneself out of love is the most terrible deception; it is an eternal loss for which there is no reparation either in time or in eternity."

I'd like to suggest, though, that we can't continue the requirement of clerical celibacy much longer. I'm talking here about the celibacy demanded of those who aren't called to the common life, specifically diocesan priests. In our church we already have married priests from some of the Eastern Rites as well as clergy who came to us from Protestant denominations. Our church, for example, has allowed Episcopalian priests who didn't agree with their church's decision to ordain women to become Catholic priests. Not every Episcopalian priest, of course, who becomes a Catholic priest disagrees with women but that seems to be the original impetus for accepting them. I believe our church must allow other married priests. Too much hinges on the sacramental nature of our church for us to prefer no priests to married priests.

Carlo Carretto asks some legitimate questions in his book, *I Sought and I Found:*

> Between an obligatory celibacy reducing the number of priests and the need to have the community without

the Eucharist, which is the right choice to make? Hasn't the community a right to the Eucharist? Why deny it to them because they have no celibate willing to be a priest?

I don't know the solutions to our increasing priest shortage but there obviously needs to be more discussion about how to continue our church's sacramental nature into the future.

Making clerical celibacy optional wouldn't cure all our priestly problems but I think it would help in a number of ways. Perhaps women would no longer be regarded primarily as "temptations" but rather as fellow pilgrims. We might be able to overcome the traditional bias against women which has had such a devastating impact on our church's history. Look, for instance, at what St. Jerome had to say about women:

> Jerome thought it best to have as little traffic with women as possible and certainly no sexual relationship, even in marriage. If a man was so craven and weak-willed that he yielded to sexual desire, then, as Jerome suggested to one correspondent, he might do better to keep his sweetheart as a concubine rather than to marry her. After all, he declared ironically, your union with a wife may prevent you from receiving holy orders when you finally come to your senses, whereas a dalliance with a concubine will not. (From *Law, Sex and Christian Society in Medieval Europe* by James A. Brundage.)

Fashioning a Healthier Religion

What kind of "saintly" advice is that? And yet there are more than a few priests who cynically advise "Do anything but don't marry her!" Jerome's attitude continues to molest our church.

We make it exceptionally difficult for a priest who wants to marry to do so. We subject him to a humiliating process known as "laicization." The priest seeking a "return to the lay state" in order to validly marry in the church must answer a very probing questionnaire about his personal life. And even if the priest goes along with the entire process, he'll most often be refused a laicization under the present papal administration.

The exception is for priests who admit pedophiliac tendencies. They're quickly granted laicizations. With priests petitioning for a laicization in order to marry, the normal denial of the petition assumes the priest will eventually "come to his senses" and return to his priestly role. We treat the priest wanting to marry as a "love-struck" adolescent, not as a man.

We've made leaving the priesthood such a trauma that many stay who probably shouldn't. Yet it doesn't help either the church or God to have embittered men charged with proclaiming the joyful love of the Father's kingdom. I don't understand why we try to disgrace priests wishing to marry. It strikes me as mean-spirited.

We continue to reap the harvest of our seminary

training. What we learned in the seminary of the past was obedience, forged in the furnace of fear. We lived in constant fear of being expelled if we didn't do as we were told. And while a healthy sense of rebelliousness existed in many of us, we became pretty obedient. I'm talking here about the high school and college seminaries of the past. I'm not knowledgeable enough about present seminary systems to say much about them. But I know my classmates and I, along with all who preceded us through our seminary halls, were conditioned to be fearfully obedient.

That fear remains alive within the souls of many of us who are ordained, making us ineffective as priests and pastors. We can't be "other Christs" if we're wrapped in fear. As Nolan claims in *Jesus Before Christianity:* "There are no traces of fear in Jesus . . . He was not afraid of creating a scandal or losing his reputation or even losing his life." So much anger and rage grows in the hothouse of fear that we cannot continue the compassionate work of Christ unless we're willing to slay most of the fears stalking us. Handicapped with the baggage of excessive fears, we won't be able to undertake the journey awaiting us. We won't be people of much faith. "Faith," as Heschel reminds us, "is an endless pilgrimage of the heart."

There are, of course, many courageous priests fighting a multitude of battles for the well-being of their people. There are many heroic priests struggling to

116

assist those "discarded" by our society. Priests in every country have willingly shed their life's blood for the sake of fuller freedom and more humane conditions. Priests have long championed people's rights.

Where we falter is not so much in the social justice arena as in the arena of love. We fear the "nakedness" necessary for love, the personal revelation lying at the core of loving. Maybe we're afraid where love will lead us. We don't visualize our lives as a "love story."

Look, for instance, at the clerical reaction to Andrew Greeley's novels. I've heard many priests carry on sarcastically about the love stories of Greeley. While jealousy seems to be at the heart of most of the sarcasm, I wonder why priests wouldn't cherish these love stories from one of our own. I'm very taken with them. *The Rite of Spring* and *The Cardinal Virtues*, for instance, have stunned me with their sense of the sacred. Greeley is absolutely correct in believing the love which God has for us is best symbolized by the love we have for each other.

A good friend of mine in the parish where I work is a Greeley "fan." She purchases Greeley's novels soon after publication and lets me read them after her (apologies for not buying my own copies). I share her enthusiasm not only because the stories are entertaining but also because they are theologically insightful. Yet his novels are sometimes dismissed by priests as being "erotic" as if eros was an enemy of life.

117

Thomas Aldworth

Greeley's novels remind me of what Teilhard de Chardin told us in *Phenomenon of Man:* "At what moment do lovers come into the most complete possession of themselves, if not when they are lost in each other?" The Scriptures continually speak of the love God has for his people as a "spousal" love, the love existing between lovers. This "lover's love" also exists between Christ and his church. How could we fail to be touched by tales of spousal love?

Yet instead of the spousal love between Christ and his church, we sometimes get side-tracked by a "maternal" love. Instead of the unconditional love of the Father for his children, we get caught in the conditional love of "Mother Church." "Mother Church" seems to be willing to love us only if we're "good" and do what she tells us. We have a hard time envisioning the spousal love of Christ for his church because "Mother" gets in the way. Rather than Kierkegaard's "dizziness of freedom," we experience instead the headache of unquestioned obedience and submission of will.

A similar dynamic happens when children are told by their parents that God won't love them unless they're obedient boys and girls. The fourth commandment's "*honor* your father and mother" gets twisted into "*obey* your father and mother." I suspect many of us were told God would "get us" if we didn't do what our parents demanded.

118

Fashioning a Healthier Religion

Alice Miller has written extensively about how children lose their sense of self when they're made submissive to their parents' will. When a child, for instance, learns that only certain feelings and actions are acceptable to mother, that her love is conditional upon acting a certain way, then the child does what's expected. He or she does whatever's demanded by the person or persons most crucial to the child's survival. Miller discusses what she terms "poisonous pedagogy" which "attempts to suppress all vitality, creativity, and feeling in the child and maintains the autocratic, godlike position of the parents at all costs." Miller contends that if people are to regain their lost sense of self, they must at some point in their lives rebel against parents' "I know better" and "I'm always right" attitudes.

It's the same with those of us serving "Mother Church." We must stand against the unhealthy demands of blind obedience and any official attitude of "I know what is best for you." If priests are going to help liberate people, we must constantly battle against whatever seeks to destroy the self or the soul. If we only feel fear when dealing with Mother Church's authority figures, then our own authority will be ineffective.

Many of us who survived the "old" seminary system had a healthy rebelliousness as part of our personality. We were able to endure the foolishness of the seminary by judiciously disregarding certain rules and regulations. Unfortunately, that healthy rebelliousness has often degenerated into a generic resentment as we progressed through our ministerial life. We decided early on not to "rock the boat" because of subsequent turmoil. We got tired of people writing complaining letters to the bishop or the pope. Many of us have gotten "punch drunk" and have wound up drifting aimlessly on a sea of cynicism.

Of course, one should pick fights prudently. Some things are worth fighting for. Some are not. If we battle everything, we'll wind up exhausted very early on. If we want to go the distance, we'll need to conserve our strength for those fights that need to be fought. Sometimes our opponent may appear easily conquered. Other times our opponent may be quite intimidating.

I remember the first Taekwondo tournament I competed in. The first fellow I was to fight was a veritable giant of a man. He was taller than my own 6« 4» and considerably bulkier. I kept wondering what in God's name I was doing getting ready to fight him. If there had been a way to exit gracefully, I'd have taken it. But since no graceful exit presented itself, I'd have to fight. We put on our sparring gear and stepped into the competition area.

I began the match with trembling legs and squeamish stomach. But I soon realized that his bulk, his size, kept him from being quick. While his strength was obviously greater than my own, his speed was considerably slower. The match wasn't nearly the challenge I'd expected. Happily my fear of appearing a coward had kept me from avoiding the fight.

When I was little, a bully lived across the alley from our house. He was a few years older than me. One winter's day my twin brother and I built a snow fort in our backyard. Pouring water on it, it became an ice fort. It'd last almost as long as winter. But the bully across the alley was apparently jealous of our fort. He came into our yard with a crowbar and destroyed it.

I cried but there was little I could do. The bully was too big for me. My big brother, though, went over to the bully's house and put considerable fear into him. The bully didn't bother us again. Perhaps parish priests need to help people deal with the bullies still abounding in our world. We must become "big brothers," battling anything or anyone seeking to strip dignity from ourselves or our people.

Those of us who work in parishes need to make those parishes places where people feel they belong. That's admittedly difficult given the size of many parishes. The parish I presently pastor has over 3,000 families as members. Yet we need to do what we can to create an atmosphere where everyone feels "at home." Our parishes can be places of loving tolerance where people embrace each other despite religious dif-

121

ferences. Our parishes can be places where no one feels rejected. While our discussions about God and religion might become heated, that heat doesn't cool into animosity.

Our parishes ideally promote lively dialogue, encouraging people to think for themselves. Yet many parish priests feel so harried that they've little time or energy available for such lively dialogue. Not wanting our people to go "wrong," we caution them to stay on the well-worn but sometimes humdrum paths of the past. We often feed our people the most bland spiritual food, afraid of causing indigestion with an occasional dash of tabasco.

I try to bring in "outside" priests and preachers on a regular basis to the parish. It'd be egotistical assuming I possess all the nourishment our parish needs. I've also "traded pulpits" with local ministers. Such "trading" is a visible sign of ecumenism and a source of healing in the Christian community. I confess there's nothing more thrilling than preaching in an African-American Baptist or A.M.E. church. The encouragement given by such congregations makes preaching there a true taste of paradise.

Preaching is often where we priests fail our people the most. I'm amazed at the theology proclaimed from pulpits. I don't get many opportunities to hear other priests since I'm usually preaching myself. But those times that I've been "in the pews" have made me sad at what people endure in Sunday sermons. I remember not long ago listening to a sermon in St. Louis. The priest was proclaiming how good God was to have kept it from raining on the parish carnival the previous day. While God had supposedly kept away the rain from the parish carnival, he'd also flooded half of Missouri. What kind of God would keep rain away from a parish carnival while unleashing watery destruction elsewhere? I'm sure the priest didn't intend to present such an immature portrait of God. He probably didn't bother pondering the logical conclusions of his homily. That's a common malady among those of us who preach.

I suspect a good number of priests and deacons use a homily service for their Sunday preaching. A homily service provides pre-fashioned homilies pertinent to the readings of a given weekend. I've written a few of these homilies myself. Such services are beneficial to priests and deacons, providing useful insights into the readings. These "packaged" homilies usually present well-developed theology, coupled with suitable stories.

The problems inherent in these homily services, though, are two-fold. The first problem is that the homilies are written in a generic way. They can't be written very personally lest they be unusable to others. If a priest or deacon just repeats what the homily service says, there will be little that is per-

Thomas Aldworth

sonal in the preaching. It won't reflect the experience
of the person giving the homily, which is a most vital
ingredient. As Ralph Waldo Emerson told people at
the Harvard Divinity School in the last century: "The
true preacher can be known by this, that he deals
out to the people his life—life passed through the
fire of thought." If priests and ministers don't "deal
out" their own life to people, then they've refused
to pastor them. We can normally only lead people
to places we've already been.

A second problem that can occur when a priest
or deacon relies solely on homily helps is that he may
abdicate his responsibility to read. I certainly know
that parish priests are often quite busy. But to stop
reading is an injustice to the people we serve. It's
like a physician. Who'd want to be in the hands of
a doctor who hadn't kept abreast of current medical
trends and discoveries? It's the same with priests.
If we don't read, we'll have to rely on what we learned in the perhaps distant past. We'll have nothing
refreshing to offer. And since our theology would
be unchallenged by new perspectives, we'd have no
reason seeking "new" truths. We'd continue offering "stale" food to our hungry parishioners. Those
who dared question our antiquated theology would
be judged trouble-makers rather than co-explorers.

While homily helps can be beneficial, too often
they're used as a convenient way of escaping Scrip-

tural self-confrontation. We don't have to allow the Sunday readings to serve as a mirror, enabling us to examine our faith and our flaws. The more often we conduct such an examination, the more accepting we'll be of everyone who is faith-full and flawed.

We priests have great power. Even in these days of priestly pedophilia and scandals, people still have great respect for us. Some people, of course, feel threatened, projecting onto priests all manner of guilt and unresolved "father" issues. But, by and large, we're still esteemed by the people in our parishes.

Some priests, though, claim to be over-worked and under-valued. Some protest what they regard as less affirmation in priesthood today. While there may be less affirmation now than previously, I get a bit agitated with priestly demands for affirmation. I think of my father loading freight cars for the Baltimore and Ohio Railroad. I think of my mother slaving away as a servant during her first years in America. I think of my two brothers working for Amoco. We priests don't always appreciate the lack of affirmation in the normal work-a-day world. Job affirmation is a rarity everywhere.

We priests are often too quick with our answers. When people come to us with a dilemma, we too easily tell them what they should do. We discard their options with seemingly infallible dictates about

Thomas Aldworth

what is best for them. We often allow little time or freedom to discuss options, treating people as perpetual children. We presume to know what is best for them, which probably does more damage to us than to our parishioners. We are people's servant, not their savior.

Priests are easily "infected" with authoritarianism. It's difficult not being infected at least occasionally. When I'm pressed for time, it's often easier just to give an answer, a pronouncement. Non-directive counseling is hard work. Allowing people to evolve their own decisions requires patience. It's a patience I don't always possess.

There are, of course, times when direct answers are called for. There's nothing wrong with deciding quickly what should be done about the faulty plumbing. But we pastors make so many decisions concerning the physical aspects of our parish "plant" that we sometimes treat complicated human decisions in the same way. Yet every time I command people what choice to make, I diminish their freedom and weaken their self-esteem.

This diminishment of freedom can be seen in something as trivial as demanding where people should sit. I've heard of priests who turn off lights in the back of their church, trying to force people to sit up front. I've heard of priests who rope off sections of church so people have no choice where to sit. And while subscribing to the social/communal dimension of Eucharist, I think we should let people sit where they want. We would well remember that priestly petulance is not a virtue.

Priests would also do well to examine their sense of humor, particularly self-humor. One can often tell how fragile people's egos are by seeing if they can laugh at themselves. We often take ourselves so seriously. If we can learn to laugh at ourselves, we'll be able to treat people with a lighter touch. Recalling Augustine's assertion that "we are set free by the foolishness of God," we should reflect at least a trace of that divine foolishness. Playing the fool joyfully is probably one of the more consistent saintly traits. To freely admit our foolishness may help our parishioners appreciate God's foolishness. Faith is often brewed in the distillery of foolishness. And such foolish faith is always evidenced by joy. Yet how many priests are inflamed with joy?

The truth is many of us may be a bit jealous of joy. The reality of this jealousy confronted me one August day, 1990, in the Slovenian resort of Portroz. Having just completed a month-long Franciscan study pilgrimage in Rome and Assisi, I went wandering. I wound up in the lovely Adriatic town of Portroz. I spent a week there, soaking in the sunshine and trying to communicate as best I could in my rusty German and ghastly Italian.

Thomas Aldworth

One evening I was in the plaza, drinking a beer
and listening to a band play songs from the Sixties.
I was watching a man and woman dance with great
glee when it suddenly dawned on me that I was
jealous of them. I was jealous of their joy. As I
observed this exuberant couple clearly enjoying each
other, I could barely contain my envy. While I'd seen
couples delight in each other over the years, it was
in Portroz that I acknowledged how jealous of joy
I really was. I was jealous of people relishing each
other, of exulting in another.

I'm not sure where the jealousy came from. Maybe
the suspicions of the female planted in the seminary
had sprouted into jealousy. Maybe the dread of intimacy indoctrinated into me had sublimated into
an envy of ecstasy. I'm not sure how the jealousy
evolved but once I acknowledged its existence, I was
able to make adjustments. I could finally share in
the couple's joy. Emotions like jealousy, anger and
fearfulness grow only when they're denied. Once
their existence is admitted, they lose much of their
power. So it was with my jealousy.

I've a sneaky suspicion that some of our priestly
over-concern with sexual sins springs from a similar
jealousy of joy. Preaching shame and guilt, we make
feelings of joy awfully hard to experience. The joy
of a Francis of Assisi, for instance, is so refreshing
because our church so often promotes a joylessness

128

Fashioning a Healthier Religion

rooted in an obsession with sin. A joyful spirit shatters the judgmental arrogance often contaminating our rectories and religious houses.

Being a priest today is tough but we should realize people expect us to be prayerful pilgrims, not perfected gurus. Priesthood brings with it moments of excruciating loneliness as well as moments of exquisite fulfillment. We touch people's lives at times of crushing pain and dazzling jubilation. There are more wonderful moments in priesthood than in any other profession I know of. There are, of course, moments not so wonderful.

I remember the time I discovered a dead cat lying in front of our church in Grambling, Louisiana. I decided it might go away by itself if I ignored it. I hoped a neighborhood vulture would come and gobble it up. I assumed pastoring a church didn't include dealing with dead cats. But I was wrong!

That Saturday evening, after our liturgy, one of the parishioners informed me that we had a dead cat on our front lawn. I already knew we had a dead cat on our lawn but now I would have to do something about it. I could no longer claim ignorance, a strategy which had served me well in the past. So I went out later that night with two plastic baggies. One baggie was for the cat. The other was to serve as a glove to handle the cat. No telling what kind of creepy things stake claim to a dead cat!

129

Thomas Aldworth

When I got to the cat, I realized this was no ordinary-size cat. This was a really big cat or else death had considerably inflated him (by now I realized it was a "him"). I grabbed his tail with my baggie glove and lifted him from his temporary resting place. But as I picked him up, his tail came off in my hand! This cat was rapidly returning to the dust from whence it came.

I grabbed what was left and shoved the remains into the baggie. Then leading a solitary procession to the trash can, I unceremoniously dropped him into it. It wasn't the most decent burial but it was better than decomposing on our church lawn. Being a priest/pastor isn't all delightful moments!

It's admittedly painful living without the exclusive love of another. Early morning doubts sometimes make me wonder if I've chosen the most loving path. Late night uncertainties make me question if I'm a priest because of narcissistic hungers. I do know, though, that priesthood is a place where my own brokenness empowers me to be of service. I've come to grasp in my middle years the truth Eugene Kennedy states in his novel, *Fixes:* "Love is God's gift to the wounded . . . nobody else would recognize it."

CHAPTER SIX

Final Reflections

WHEN I was very young, hardly able to walk, I learned that life isn't always fair. My mother had brought my twin brother and me to have our first formal picture taken. When we got to the studio, probably at some place like Sears, my twin brother began to cry. Because he was crying, the photographer gave him a small stuffed dog. My brother stopped crying but I sat there stunned. Why did my brother, who was being "bad," get a stuffed dog when I, who was being good as gold, got nothing? The dog, of course, was taken away as soon as the photo was snapped. But I still look at that photo on my office desk and see my brother's smiling face as he squeezes his stuffed dog. Peering into my own eyes, I see an infantile awareness that the world isn't always fair.

In some ways we use God as an "escape clause" for the world's inherent unfairness/injustice. Bad guys prosper but God will get them in the end. Good people suffer but God will eventually reward them. God is fashioned from our hopes that everything will be all right as the final curtain descends. And we need such a satisfactory conclusion if we're to be believers. As Albert Nolan concludes in *Jesus Before Christianity:*

> To believe in God is to believe that goodness is more powerful than evil and truth is more powerful than falsehood. To believe in God is to believe that in the end goodness and truth will triumph over evil and falsehood. Anyone who thinks that evil will have the last word or that good and evil have a fifty-fifty chance is an atheist.

The world, however, does appear untrustworthy. I believe this sense of "untrustworthiness" to be one of the main evils confronting our world. Because of this untrustworthiness, we've lived over four decades in the shadow of nuclear annihilation. Because of this untrustworthiness, we use drugs to silence the pains inflicted in our attempts to trust. Labeling ourselves "realists," we try to make it in our world as best we can. We snicker at innocence and delight in the telltale tabloids. We come to church more for our children than for ourselves. Our trust has been so battered that we really don't know about this God who's supposed to be running things.

God must, obviously, be about trust. His grace is the glue mending our broken trust. We experience the freedom of God's children when we're able to trust in an untrustworthy world. When we choose to trust, we wage war against the fears assailing our souls. When we trust, we become capable of love. Love may primarily be the ability to trust fully in another. When trust is gone, so is love.

While it's hard trusting today, it's probably always been a rare commodity. Perhaps the intrinsic loss of trust which comes with living is the true "original sin." Maybe Jesus saved us by trusting even in the midst of betrayal and death. Resurrection might be the reward for complete trust in the Father. Faith and trust seem to be identical twins, having the same parents and arising from the same egg.

The Brazilian Leonardo Boff suggests in *Saint Francis, Model of Liberation:* "The root of our cultural crisis resides in the terrifying lack of gentleness and care for each other, of nature and of the future." This "lack of gentleness and care" is coupled with a growing inability to trust. We've become people with so many fears that trust becomes psychologically and spiritually unavailable to us.

There are at least two causes for this growing inability to trust. The first centers on nuclear armaments. How can we trust in the future when the future is so uncertain? While the threat of nuclear destruction has diminished because of recent world events, the threat continues to stalk our world. What happens in the hearts and minds of children when they learn their lives might be extinguished in a nuclear conflagration? Doesn't an uncertain future necessarily produce a narcissistic orientation to immediate pleasure?

Thomas Aldworth

One of the more important psychological dimensions is the ability to delay gratification. When we're able to delay gratification for the sake of others or for the sake of our own growth, then we're developing in a mature manner. When we cannot delay gratification, we stop growing. Yet many of us who have grown up under the nuclear cloud have a hard time delaying gratification.

The other cause of the increasing failure to trust involves how much we see and hear from an early age. As we move from infancy to childhood, we need to see our world as a primarily trustworthy place. Yet sitting in front of our televisions, we see all the horrors inflicted on our world. We're constantly bombarded with violence and mayhem. It's improbable becoming trusting people in the midst of all the darkness poured over our heads and hearts.

We've grown accustomed to being afraid. We're afraid the person passing us on the street is a serial killer. We're afraid the baby-sitter or day care worker is a child molester. We're afraid drug-crazies will burglarize our home to finance their next drug buy. Trust has seemingly become a dispensable commodity. We can make do without it. If we're trusting, we're liable to be robbed, raped or killed. And so we walk our city streets, making sure not to catch the eyes of those walking with us lest they explode into some sort of maniacal frenzy. We see rage rampaging like a hurricane around us so we batten down the hatches, trying to ride out the storm.

Finding God in our bruised and battered world is a prodigious task. Many continue using God as a weapon against others. We all know about the millions of lives sacrificed on the altars of religious intolerance. People continue to believe the world would be a better place if everyone was a Christian or a Moslem or a Hindu or a Jew or a Buddhist. Many Christians believe the world would be better if everyone was a Catholic or a Southern Baptist or a Methodist or a "Bible-believer" or a "Spirit-filled." Such beliefs serve as the breeding ground for religious intolerance and hatred.

Religion has to do with rules. Religions are, after all, ethical ways of approaching life. The great religions have each produced a correspondent morality. The original moral visions continue to create hopes and dreams. Religious images continue to sustain our human aspirations.

I don't believe the future would be a better place without religion. We need religions to prosper. But they can only prosper in an atmosphere of human values and healthy theology. Those of us who are the "torchbearers" of religion should spend less energy defending the past and more energy rescuing the present.

We'd do well, of course, to explore the past, studying the wisdom of our heritage. The saints and mystics who have traveled the way of Jesus these past two thousand years have left us a colossal legacy of truth. "Knowledge of self without knowledge of God leads to despair," for instance, is as true today as when Bernard of Clairvaux said it in the 12th century.

There are many ways to come to God. We who have the task of assisting people choose a "God path" need to realize that many paths exist. We do people a disservice telling them they must only travel this path or that. We do them a disservice insisting which guidebook they should carry on their journey.

Admittedly, some of the ways people tried to come to God in the past strike us as strange today. Richard Woods in *Christian Spirituality: God's Presence Through the Ages* talks about some of these strange approaches:

> Dendrites and Stylites achieved physical and spiritual heights in tiny cells atop trees and columns. Adamites disdained the protection (and modesty) of even minimal clothing. Other ascetics remained standing for prolonged periods, such as Lent, and in some instances on one foot alone. Many eschewed ever washing themselves or their clothing (more often animal hides), suffering skin diseases and the incessant attack of vermin as part of the cost of discipleship.

We may consider such ascetics to be crazy yet the physical abuse they endured may have helped them experience the transcendence we all seek. Research has shown that under extreme stress the brain produces neuro-transmitters which cause people to perceive reality in altered ways.

Humans may have a genetic need to experience transcendence in their lives. Perhaps that's the fatal attraction of drugs, as William James suggested many years ago. Perhaps when our religions don't help us feel one with all life, the need may be so compelling that we're easy prey to the sway of drugs.

I'm not suggesting the religious experiences of the mystics and ascetics only resulted from neuro-transmitters. If God is our creator, as I believe, then he's the one who has fashioned our brains as they are. He's the one who seems to have "wired" us with a longing for transcendence, a hunger for him. The "restless heart" of Augustine may result from a physiological need the Creator planted within us as we evolved into consciousness. The creature needs to know the Creator. We, who are made, keep searching for our Maker. But we discover the truth of Isaiah 45:15, "Truly you are a God who hides yourself."

Why does God hide from us? God's silence during the Nazi holocaust still unnerves me. His hiding in the face of Cambodia's "killing fields" is hard to comprehend. There must be some good reason why God remains hidden. I'm not sure, though, what that reason might be. We should be cautious in providing simplistic or pietistic "alibis" for God.

Thomas Aldworth

Even though God conceals himself from us, we have some idea about what God calls us to be and do. By immersing ourselves in the Gospels of Jesus, we'll become familiar with the kingdom dream of Jesus' Father. That kingdom is the place where all are made to feel welcome. That kingdom is the place where all are loved. That kingdom is the place where everyone's dignity is vividly apparent.

Another way to understand this kingdom dream is through prayer. As Heschel reminds us: "To pray is to dream in league with God, to envision his holy visions." While many of us spend our prayer time delivering requests, perhaps we should spend some time assimilating our Father's dreams. God is constantly dreaming his dream of the kingdom to come.

I wish I'd been given this hope-filled image of God the Dreamer when I was a child, rather than the image of God the ill-tempered Destroyer. I'd have rejoiced in a God who was the source of all dreams worth dreaming. While our fears and failures generate nightmares, God is continually calling us back to the dream, to hope, to faith. Maybe faith is the willingness to let God's dream envelop our souls. Maybe faith is the trust that prepares a place for God's dream to live within our hearts.

Many things keep us from dreaming God's dreams. Sometimes the fears fashioned by faulty religious training make us too frightened to sleep the dreamer's sleep. Sometimes we've been anesthetized to God's dream by an over-emphasis on the world to come, trapped in a dreamless sleep by the sedative of personal salvation. Since we've been taught to be principally concerned with our own salvation, we get caught in a narcissistic spirituality unable to sustain the expansive dream of the prophets and the Messiah.

Much of the spirituality we've been raised with generates a faith-life too narrow and individualistic. Through a preoccupation with hell-fire and punishment, we've created a faith seriously compressed by fear. There's little hope for faith to unfold when fear crushes it. And while faith is stronger than fear, faith mingled with fear loses much of its power. I was given such fear-mingled faith when I was young. I don't, however, blame the Sisters or priests who influenced my faith-development. They could only teach me what they themselves had been taught.

We who fashion the faith-life of our children, need to exorcise the demons that were part of our own religious upbringing. We can't frighten our children with devils and hell-fire if we want them to have any possibility of dreaming the Father's dream. We can't give them a narcissistic view of salvation if we want them to work for the coming of the kingdom. We can't weaken them with fears if we expect them to have the courage required to wrestle the enemies of life and the enemies of the kingdom-dream.

Thomas Aldworth

I remember the excitement that seized me the day of Dr. Martin Luther King's "I Have A Dream" speech. I still can't listen to that speech without tears welling-up in my eyes. While we have come to know Dr. King's human wounds, the authority of his words continues to haunt us. I believe his words still haunt us because within each of us there's a place where dreams are planted. Perhaps our soul is the field where dreams are sown. God's grace waters the dream-seeds into harvest. But such fields can't be fertile if they're filled with the rocks of fear and fear-spawned prejudices.

I recall the times I've gone to my father's birthplace in the hills of southwest Ireland. My father was born and raised in the charming town of Sneem on the magical Ring of Kerry. My father's tiny family farm was basically one rock piled on top of another. Little could grow there. A few scrawny sheep wandered the barren hillsides. While there was a rugged beauty to the place, it wasn't a place of great productivity.

Many of us, I fear, are like my father's family farm. Many of us have our inner fields littered with the rocks of intolerance and enmity. Our souls are strewn with the boulders of bigotry. And so there's work to do. We need to help each other clear away the rocks and boulders that are scattered across our fields. We need to be reminded, though, that the rocks aren't from our Father. He doesn't go around dumping rocks into his children's fields. The rocks get pushed into our fields when we're given fear instead of faith. The rocks remain as long as we're frightened of losing the Father's love because of our sinfulness.

We who serve the church need to help people remove their rocks through love and compassion, through forgiveness and understanding. We need to alter our theology from a "sin theology" to a "love theology." I realize I may sound like a left-over "hippy" or a clericalized version of Leo Buscaglia. Yet I've lived long enough to realize that love is the dream God dreams. I believe love is the passion which empowers peace and justice. I believe love is the only truth that sets us free. I believe love is the sole entree for our eschatological/eternal banquet.

Loving carries a considerable price-tag but not loving is like declaring bankruptcy. Our church needs to sensitize us to the opportunities for loving behavior in our lives. Our church needs to reveal to us the "warm breast" and "bright wings" immortalized by Gerard Manley Hopkins. Our church needs to be "like shining from shook foil." Otherwise our young won't see in our parish communities the way of love at work in our world. They'll see the hypocrisy inherent in institutional structures and not glimpse how we're striving to enflesh the "love-dream" of our Father. We won't appear to them as the fertile fields of Kansas but, rather, the craggy fields of Kerry.

Thomas Aldworth

Our church needs to recognize the role she's been given. She's neither the source of light nor life. She reflects the One who is light and life. But the church, like the moon, is of great assistance. We can't look directly into the sun without becoming blind. We grasp a sense of the sun's brilliance through the mirror of the moon. The "brightness" of God is too much for us to gaze upon with human eyes. That's why God in Hebrew thought was surrounded by the presence called the "Shekinah." The Shekinah was the cloud which "obscured" the majesty of God. If a person gazed at the full radiance of God, he or she would die. But one could safely enter the Shekinah since one would then be looking at God through the Shekinah's obscuring "haze."

Our church serves as a mirror, enabling us to glimpse the reflected likeness of God. We sense God's brilliance through the reflected mirroring of the church. Our task as church is to continually polish ourselves so the image reflected will be a trustworthy one. We saw how a minuscule flaw in the Hubbard Space telescope's mirror made the telescope virtually useless. It's the same thing with our church. We who comprise the church need to acknowledge our flaws so we can polish them away. A perfect mirror, of course, like a perfect vacuum, exists only in theory. But we shouldn't despair of the task before us. Perhaps the full coming of the kingdom will occur when the reflected image of the Father becomes a faithful one.

About ten years ago, I underwent Jungian analysis. It was a long and painful process of self-reflection and discovery. Having been encouraged to undergo the process because of M. Scott Peck's first book, *The Road Less Traveled*, I found an analyst who was also an Episcopalian priest. We spent many hours together, searching for the half-buried griefs that littered the graveyard of my memories.

At the end of our two years together, I told him he'd served a significant purpose in my life. He'd acted as a mirror for me to see the reflection of my own identity. But towards the end of our time together, he was no longer a mirror. He'd become a window for me to look out unto the world. Perhaps the task of our church is to serve as a mirror not only for us to see God's reflection but also for us to see our true self. Such is the church's task until that time when she's transformed from a mirror into a window, allowing us to gaze fully on the face of God.

Our church's job is to bring us to that place where we meet God. We, who serve the church as leaders, need to be experienced guides, bringing our people to the meeting place, the rendezvous point. But in serving as guides, we should heed Thomas Aquinas' admonition: ''God is the most truly simple thing there is. One comes to God and departs from him not by

Thomas Aldworth

bodily movement, since he is everywhere, but by movement of the heart." We who are "God- guides," therefore, must become heart specialists. We require a working knowledge of the mysteries of the heart. Without such knowledge, we only take people for a ride rather than a rendezvous.

Seeking to come to God by "movement of the heart," we'd do well to explore the feelings we have for ourselves and others. As Merle Shain reminds us in her final book, *Courage My Love:* "Our loved ones carry the burden of how we feel about ourselves." When we try to love others, we bring not only our love but also our self-image. And since many of us have damaged self-images, love is more mirage than reality. Perhaps God's supreme love bears the burden of our distorted and damaged self-images.

We who are God-guides need to help people discard their excess baggage. When I travel, I normally bring one carry-on bag. I'm often amazed at what people drag with them on trips. Maybe people feel less vulnerable with their things surrounding them but excess baggage prevents fast and comprehensive travel. The best way to travel is do so lightly. We who serve our people need to help them lighten their loads, taking from their shoulders the baggage of punitive God-images and unhealthy sin beliefs.

It's not only punitive God-images which can weigh us down. We can also be crushed under sweetness-

and-light portrayals of God: God as a totally permissive and indulgent father. Such "cotton candy" images serve to make us feel better about ourselves without challenging us to do something about the world in which we live.

When we see the enormous problems facing our world we easily become "shell-shocked." Such tremendous difficulties confront us that we may occasionally want to avoid all news. We may want a respite from all the crises constantly screaming at us. We may shout "Leave me alone!" But even though we can't always do a great deal, we still need to make some offering to the problems of our world. We need to offer our "widow's mite."

I remember when my classmates and I received what is known as "tonsure." We were the last class to undergo this very old tradition. The tonsure ceremony signified a seminarian's entrance into the clerical life. The bishop would cut five pieces of hair from the seminarian's head, snipping the pieces from four corners in the sign of the cross. One of my classmates had almost no hair covering the top of his head. He knelt down before the bishop and bowed his head, awaiting tonsure. The bishop, looking down at the shiny head before him, began to smile. He glanced up at us and proclaimed with good-natured grace "The widow's mite!" While we've limited resources for alleviating the world's

Thomas Aldworth

afflictions, we always have our "widow's mite."

I believe our widow's mite is simply the insistence on caring, our continued attempt to share the joys and sorrows of others. Our willingness to care may be both the true test of being a Christian and the true test of being human. Rollo May offers this definition: "the ability to care is the refusal to accept emptiness though you face it on every side; the dogged insistence on human dignity, though it be violated on every side." If we don't care, we'll become careless, constantly stepping on and tripping over others.

The careful way is not the way of indulgence or pain-free existence. To care is to suffer with. To care is to walk bravely through the pain and woe of our world, refusing to pretend that suffering is an illusion. To care is to open our arms to God and all his creation, knowing he'll bless our vulnerability and empathy. We then understand what Henri Nouen tells us in *Reaching Out:*

> It would be just another illusion to believe that reaching out to God will free us from pain and suffering. Often, indeed, it will take us where we would rather not go. But we know that without going there we will not find our life.

To care or not to care is the primary life-choice we make. The decision to care brings bruises but choosing not to care brings emptiness.

Fashioning a Healthier Religion

To care means we pay attention to the voice of the One who's calling us. I remember as a child that we never went to our friends' front doors. If we wanted to play with someone, we'd go to the back door and shout our friend's name "Yo, Johnny . . . Yo, Johnny!" If one of my friends wanted to play with me, he or she would come to my back door and shout "Yo, Tommy . . . Yo, Tommy!" None of us ever rang the doorbell. It didn't matter what floor our friend might live on. We just shouted louder for the second and third floors!

God stands outside our back doors, calling us to come out and play. Maybe we don't hear him so well because there's so much noise in our homes. Maybe we just don't care enough to listen for his call. Caring clears our ears. We begin hearing sounds outside the chatter of our own egos. Some of us may even have damaged hearing, requiring a hearing aid. Those who minister need to help fashion hearing aides for those who need them. We should do everything in our power to help people hear the voice of the One who calls all to come out and play.

Yet even if we hear our name being called, we may be too frightened to respond. We're not sure if God is really our friend or the neighborhood bully. Professional ministers need to exemplify the courage required to "come out and play." And if we don't understand the reason for courage, then we don't know what we're being asked to do. The ''games'' God likes to play are not games for cowards.

Of course, there's more involved in responding to God's call than just listening. Sometimes we may not be able to respond because we're ''locked in.'' I recall my one and only attempt at running away from home. I was ten years old. Feeling the misunderstanding common to ten-year-olds, I decided I'd had enough. I'd run away and make everyone sorry for the ways they'd supposedly mistreated me. Bolting out the back door, I raced down the stairs from our second floor home. I was going to run through the back yard but my father was weeding. Rather than try running past him, I continued down the stairs and wound up in the basement. I hid behind the furnace's oil tank.

Shortly afterwards, I heard people looking for me. My father came into the basement, calling my name. I crouched silently behind the oil tank. My father left. I waited for awhile and then went to the door to resume my runaway. But the basement door, which was usually left open, was now padlocked. I was trapped in the basement! There was no other way out. My attempt at running away was becoming a fiasco.

After a seemingly long time, I went to the front of the basement where a window faced the street. Peering through the dusty window, I saw a cousin of mine. I began to tap on the window. My cousin heard me and I was subsequently released from the basement. I was an abject flop as a run-away.

While suffering the consequences of my attempt, I knew my "failure" was also a blessing. I wouldn't have gotten very far with no money and no place to go. I felt foolish for a long time after my runaway but I knew my father had unintentionally prevented me from making a bigger fool of myself. As I ran down the back stairs, my father seemed to be in the wrong place at the wrong time. Afterwards I realized he was in exactly the right place at the right time.

I pray we'll all have such "luck" in our lives. I pray we'll have people in our lives who'll prevent us from running away from ourselves and the One who gives us life. I pray we'll have people in our lives who'll hear us as we tap on our basement windows, seeking release from the hiding places entrapping us. I pray we'll all be runaway "failures.'